studysync®

Reading & Writing Companion

The Powers that Be

studysync

studysync.com

Send all inquiries to:
BookheadEd Learning, LLC
610 Daniel Young Drive
Sonoma, CA 95476

Cover, ©iStock.com/DNY59, ©iStock.com/ER09, ©iStock.com/alexey_boldin, ©iStock.com/skegbydave

8 9 LWI 21 20 C

STUDENT GUIDE

GETTING STARTED

Welcome to the StudySync Reading and Writing Companion! In this booklet, you will find a collection of readings based on the theme of the unit you are studying. As you work through the readings, you will be asked to answer questions and perform a variety of tasks designed to help you closely analyze and understand each text selection. Read on for an explanation of each section of this booklet.

CORE ELA TEXTS

In each Core ELA Unit you will read texts and text excerpts that share a common theme, despite their different genres, time periods, and authors. Each reading encourages a closer look with questions and a short writing assignment.

1 INTRODUCTION

An Introduction to each text provides historical context for your reading as well as information about the author. You will also learn about the genre of the excerpt and the year in which it was written.

2 FIRST READ

During your first reading of each excerpt, you should just try to get a general idea of the content and message of the reading. Don't worry if there are parts you don't understand or words that are unfamiliar to you. You'll have an opportunity later to dive deeper into the text.

3 NOTES

Many times, while working through the activities after each text, you will be asked to **annotate** or **make annotations** about what you are reading. This means that you should highlight or underline words in the text and use the "Notes" column to make comments or jot down any questions you may have. You may also want to note any unfamiliar vocabulary words here.

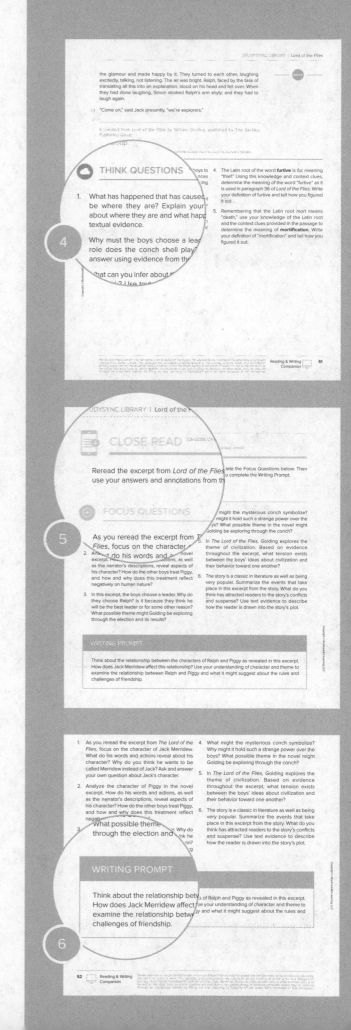

4 THINK QUESTIONS

These questions will ask you to start thinking critically about the text, asking specific questions about its purpose, and making connections to your prior knowledge and reading experiences. To answer these questions, you should go back to the text and draw upon specific evidence that you find there to support your responses. You will also begin to explore some of the more challenging vocabulary words used in the excerpt.

5 CLOSE READ & FOCUS QUESTIONS

After you have completed the First Read, you will then be asked to go back and read the excerpt more closely and critically. Before you begin your Close Read, you should read through the Focus Questions to get an idea of the concepts you will want to focus on during your second reading. You should work through the Focus Questions by making annotations, highlighting important concepts, and writing notes or questions in the "Notes" column. Depending on instructions from your teacher, you may need to respond online or use a separate piece of paper to start expanding on your thoughts and ideas.

6 WRITING PROMPT

Your study of each excerpt or selection will end with a writing assignment. To complete this assignment, you should use your notes, annotations, and answers to both the Think and Focus Questions. Be sure to read the prompt carefully and address each part of it in your writing assignment.

ENGLISH LANGUAGE DEVELOPMENT TEXTS

The English Language Development texts and activities take a closer look at the language choices that authors make to communicate their ideas. Individual and group activities will help develop your understanding of each text.

1 REREAD

After you have completed the First Read, you will have two additional opportunities to revisit portions of the excerpt more closely. The directions for each reread will specify which paragraphs or sections you should focus on.

2 USING LANGUAGE

These questions will ask you to analyze the author's use of language and conventions in the text. You may be asked to write in sentence frames, fill in a chart, or you may simply choose between multiple-choice options. To answer these questions, you should read the exercise carefully and go back in the text as necessary to accurately complete the activity.

3 MEANINGFUL INTERACTIONS & SELF-ASSESSMENT RUBRIC

After each reading, you will participate in a group activity or discussion with your peers. You may be provided speaking frames to guide your discussions or writing frames to support your group work. To complete these activities, you should revisit the excerpt for textual evidence and support. When you finish, use the Self-Assessment Rubric to evaluate how well you participated and collaborated.

EXTENDED WRITING PROJECT

The Extended Writing Project is your opportunity to explore the theme of each unit in a longer written work. You will draw information from your readings, research, and own life experiences to complete the assignment.

1 WRITING PROJECT

After you have read all of the unit text selections, you will move on to a writing project. Each project will guide you through the process of writing an argumentative, narrative, informative, or literary analysis essay. Student models and graphic organizers will provide guidance and help you organize your thoughts as you plan and write your essay. Throughout the project, you will also study and work on specific writing skills to help you develop different portions of your writing.

2 WRITING PROCESS STEPS

There are five steps in the writing process: **Prewrite**, **Plan**, **Draft**, **Revise**, and **Edit, Proofread, and Publish**. During each step, you will form and shape your writing project so that you can effectively express your ideas. Lessons focus on one step at a time, and you will have the chance to receive feedback from your peers and teacher.

3 WRITING SKILLS

Each Writing Skill lesson focuses on a specific strategy or technique that you will use during your writing project. The lessons begin by analyzing a student model or mentor text, and give you a chance to learn and practice the skill on its own. Then, you will have the opportunity to apply each new skill to improve the writing in your own project.

The Powers that Be

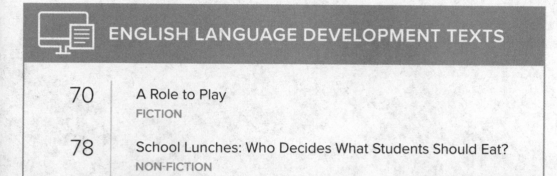

ENGLISH LANGUAGE DEVELOPMENT TEXTS

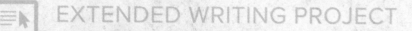

EXTENDED WRITING PROJECT

Please note that excerpts and passages in the StudySync® library and this workbook are intended as touchstones to generate interest in an author's work. The excerpts and passages do not substitute for the reading of entire texts, and StudySync® strongly recommends that students seek out and purchase the whole literary or informational work in order to experience it as the author intended. Links to online resellers are available in our digital library. In addition, complete works may be ordered through an authorized reseller by filling out and returning to StudySync® the order form enclosed in this workbook.

Reading & Writing
Companion   **3**

GLADIATOR

NON-FICTION
Richard Watkins
1997

INTRODUCTION

In the Roman Empire, gladiators entertained public audiences by violently fighting other combatants and wild animals to the death. Most gladiators had little choice over their profession—they were criminals, slaves, and war prisoners condemned to the gladiatorial arena. However, there were others that willingly chose the lifestyle; some for the promise of regular meals, and some for the promise of glory. In the following excerpt from his book, *Gladiator*, Richard Watkins describes the beginning and the end of the gladiator tradition.

"As Rome's taste for slave fights grew, so did the occasions that required them."

 FIRST READ

Chapter II: The First Gladiators

1   The first known gladiatorial combat in Rome took place at the funeral of a nobleman named Junius Brutus in 264 B.C. His sons Marcus and Decimus revived an ancient Etruscan custom of having slaves fight at the funeral of a great leader in the belief that such a sacrifice would please the gods. During the ceremony, which took place in the Forum Boarium, or cattle market, three pairs of slaves were forced to fight to the death. This strange custom grew in popularity as more rich and powerful men presented these displays as part of the ceremonies to honor their dead.

2   In 216 B.C., twenty-two pairs of slaves fought at the funeral of a man named Marcus Lepidus. Sixty pairs fought when Publicus Licinius died in 183 B.C. These slave fighters were now known as *bustiarii,* funeral men. As Rome's taste for slave fights grew, so did the occasions that required them. If a family's reputation could be enhanced by these displays, then so could a politician's chance of election or a general's popularity. It became clear that an ambitious Roman could buy a crowd's attention, ensure his social standing, and demonstrate his power over life and death.

3   By the time of Julius Caesar, any direct association with funerals and religion was gone, and these fighters, now known as gladiators, meaning swordsmen, were a powerful force in Roman politics. Caesar's genius at entertaining the masses with extravagant gladiatorial displays equaled his skills as a general and a politician. He bought the affection of the people with magnificent banquets and spectacles that were open and free to the public. He showered his political supporters and his *legionaries* (soldiers) with gold. All this gave Caesar unlimited power and established the precedent of keeping the **populace** occupied with triumphal processions, chariot races, and gladiator shows. The bigger the event, the more impressed the people were. In 46 B.C. Caesar staged a battle between two armies, each with 500 men, 30 cavalrymen, and 20 battle elephants. He topped that with a naval battle with 1,000 sailors and 2,000 oarsman, staged on a huge artificial lake dug just for that purpose.

4   These gladiatorial combats affirmed Julius Caesar's power and, to him, the cost in gold and human lives was worth it. Augustus Caesar, in 22 B.C., brought all games in Rome under his direct control, making them a state monopoly. He realized that the games were too important a political tool to be exploited by anyone else.

Chapter XI: The End of the Gladiators

5   From the first recorded gladiator fights in 264 B.C. to their final **abolition** almost seven hundred years later, countless thousands died in the arena, all victims of some of the greatest exhibitions of brutality in history. The culture that produced the gladiators also created the atmosphere that eventually led to their extinction.

6   Like all great empires, Rome reached the height of its power and then, over a long period of time, began to collapse. It became impossible to maintain the huge armies needed to protect its border from invaders, the vast number of people ruled by the empire became unmanageable, and the bureaucracy required to keep the government running became bloated and corrupt. The later emperors lacked the absolute power to demand the money and resources required to stage shows as extravagant as the ones given when Rome was at its apex.

7   Although Rome's glory faded over the centuries, Rome was still the major power of its time, and its subjects still expected to be amused by great shows. As time went on, novel acts were harder to create and exotic animals harder to obtain, and the shows became slightly less spectacular. The blood of innocent men and beasts continued to spill, however, and the crowds continued to enjoy the sight of pain and suffering.

8   It took the rise of a new faith to change the attitudes of ruler and ruled alike enough to stop gladiatorial combat. Christianity was born in the Roman Empire and found many **converts** among the poor and powerless. The pagan gods of Rome and the emperors who made themselves gods ruled the people with an attitude of total and merciless authority. These new Christians that preached peace and love often found themselves facing death in the arena when they refused to worship the emperor or his gods. The empire unknowingly aided the growth of this new faith. Every attempt to stop the spread of Christianity with the threat of **persecution** and death seemed to encourage more converts. These converts began to realize that the pain and terror inflicted in the arena was at odds with the gentle and merciful words of their new religion.

9   Christianity gained its more powerful convert in A.D. 312 when the emperor Constantine the Great adopted the faith and declared Christianity the state religion. He issued an edict abolishing gladiatorial combat in A.D. 323. This edict further stated that those condemned to the arena should serve

Copyright © BookheadEd Learning, LLC

NOTES

their sentences in the mines instead. This was a humanitarian gesture in theory only, because forced labor in the mines was nearly as deadly as combat in the arena, though far less dramatic. This ban, however, was not enforced. Constantine himself allowed several gladiator shows to be given, contradicting his own law. It is proof of the powerful attraction of the games that even a great leader like Constantine could not or would not stop them completely. Crowds still filled amphitheaters all over the empire to watch gladiators do their bloody work. Christianity needed more time to wipe out all the pagan beliefs of Rome; even some of the gladiators were Christians. It wasn't until A.D. 367 that the emperor Valentinian I stopped the condemnation of Christians to the gladiator schools. Although emperor Honorius closed the gladiator schools in A.D. 399, the games still seemed to be thriving.

10   Five years later, a tragic event finally put an end to the gladiators. In A.D. 404, a Christian monk named Telemachus jumped into an arena in Rome and tried to separate two combatants. The crowd went berserk, climbed over the walls into the arena, and tore the monk limb from limb. In response to this ugly incident, the emperor Honorius immediately and permanently banned all gladiator combats. Unlike Constantine, he enforced the law.

11   The era of the gladiator was over. Though the Roman Empire was officially a Christian state for ninety-two years before gladiators were abolished, Christianity was primarily responsible for bringing an end to gladiator combats. Violence and cruelty would continue to be all too common in history, but never again would the amphitheater fill with people gathered to watch men kill each other for sport.

 THINK QUESTIONS   CA-CCSS: CA.RI.7.1, CA.L.7.4a, CA.L.7.4d

1.   Who was responsible for the first-known combat between gladiators in Rome, and why did the custom grow? Cite specific evidence from the first paragraph of the text to support your answer.

2.   In what ways did gladiatorial combat change between the time of Julius Caesar in 46 B.C. and Constantine the Great in A.D. 312? Cite textual evidence from Chapters II and XI to support your answer.

3.   When did emperor Honorius ban all gladiatorial combat? Explain his reasons for banning all combat between gladiators and cite specific textual evidence from paragraph 10 to support your explanation.

4.   Use context to figure out the meaning of the word **converts** as it is used in sentence 2 of paragraph 8. Write your definition of "converts" and explain how you figured out the meaning.

5.   Use a print or an online dictionary to confirm the meaning of **persecution** as it is used in paragraph 8. Write the definition. Then provide evidence from the paragraph that "persecution" is being used correctly in the text.

CLOSE READ

CA-CCSS: CA.RI.7.1, CA.RI.7.5, CA.RI.7.5a, CA.W.7.2a, CA.W.7.2b, CA.W.7.2c, CA.W.7.2d, CA.W.7.2e, CA.W.7.2f, CA.W.7.4, CA.W.7.5, CA.W.7.6, CA.W.710

Reread the excerpt from *Gladiator*. As you reread, complete the Focus Questions below. Then use your answers and annotations from the questions to help you complete the Writing Prompt.

FOCUS QUESTIONS

1. As you reread the excerpt from *Gladiator*, remember that the author uses sequential text structure, or time order. Highlight the dates in *Gladiator* that reveal this text structure. Annotate why each date is significant to the rise and fall of the Roman gladiator.

2. Chapter headings (number and title of chapter) organize the text into smaller sections that help readers locate specific information. As a result, chapter headings can often provide a clue to the overarching structure of a text. Highlight the two chapter headings in this selection, and explain how they indicate that the text is organized by sequential text structure, or time order. Use annotations to support your explanation.

3. In paragraph 3, how does the author use cause-and-effect text structure to explain Julius Caesar's role in the growth of the gladiator tradition? Highlight textual evidence to support your ideas and write annotations to explain your response.

4. Highlight and annotate the text evidence in paragraph 6 that shows how the author uses cause-and-effect text structure to explain how the "culture that produced the gladiators also created the atmosphere that eventually led to their extinction."

5. What text structure does the author use in paragraph 8? How does the relationship between events help readers to infer that the converts hoped their new faith would lead them to living in a more just society? Highlight your evidence in the text and make annotations to explain your analysis.

WRITING PROMPT

Why does the author use sequence (or time order) in *Gladiator* to organize his ideas? How does telling about the events in the order that they happened help you understand what brought about the beginning and end of the gladiator tradition in Rome? Introduce your ideas clearly with a thesis statement. Use transition words and text features, such as headings or a timeline, to organize and connect your writing. Support your writing with evidence from the text and develop your ideas with facts and examples. Use precise language and maintain a formal writing style. Provide a strong conclusion to support your information.

Reading & Writing Companion

THE LOTTERY

FICTION
Shirley Jackson
1948

INTRODUCTION

When this story appeared in *The New Yorker* in 1948, the response was loud, but divided: many distressed readers wrote in to cancel their subscriptions. Others asked in which town it was modeled so they could be spectators of such an event. Called "an icon in the history of the American short story," Shirley Jackson's piece may be controversial, but once read, it engraves itself in readers' psyches forever.

"Although the villagers had forgotten the ritual...they still remembered to use stones."

 FIRST READ

1   The morning of June 27th was clear and sunny, with the fresh warmth of a full-summer day; the flowers were blossoming profusely and the grass was richly green. The people of the village began to gather in the square, between the post office and the bank, around ten o'clock; in some towns there were so many people that the **lottery** took two days and had to be started on June 26th. but in this village, where there were only about three hundred people, the whole lottery took less than two hours, so it could begin at ten o'clock in the morning and still be through in time to allow the villagers to get home for noon dinner.

2   The children assembled first, of course. School was recently over for the summer, and the feeling of liberty sat uneasily on most of them; they tended to gather together quietly for a while before they broke into boisterous play, and their talk was still of the classroom and the teacher, of books and reprimands. Bobby Martin had already stuffed his pockets full of stones, and the other boys soon followed his example, selecting the smoothest and roundest stones; Bobby and Harry Jones and Dickie Delacroix—the villagers pronounced this name "Dellacroy"—eventually made a great pile of stones in one corner of the square and guarded it against the raids of the other boys. The girls stood aside, talking among themselves, looking over their shoulders at the boys, and the very small children rolled in the dust or clung to the hands of their older brothers or sisters.

3   Soon the men began to gather, surveying their own children, speaking of planting and rain, tractors and taxes. They stood together, away from the pile of stones in the corner, and their jokes were quiet and they smiled rather than laughed. The women, wearing faded house dresses and sweaters, came shortly after their menfolk. They greeted one another and exchanged bits of gossip as they went to join their husbands. Soon the women, standing by their husbands, began to call to their children, and the children came

NOTES

reluctantly, having to be called four or five times. Bobby Martin ducked under his mother's grasping hand and ran, laughing, back to the pile of stones. His father spoke up sharply, and Bobby came quickly and took his place between his father and his oldest brother.

4   The lottery was conducted—as were the square dances, the teen club, the Halloween program—by Mr. Summers, who had time and energy to devote to civic activities. He was a round-faced, jovial man and he ran the coal business, and people were sorry for him because he had no children and his wife was a scold. When he arrived in the square, carrying the black wooden box, there was a murmur of conversation among the villagers, and he waved and called, "Little late today, folks." The postmaster, Mr. Graves, followed him, carrying a three- legged stool, and the stool was put in the center of the square and Mr. Summers set the black box down on it. The villagers kept their distance, leaving a space between themselves and the stool, and when Mr. Summers said, "Some of you fellows want to give me a hand?" there was a hesitation before two men, Mr. Martin and his oldest son, Baxter, came forward to hold the box steady on the stool while Mr. Summers stirred up the papers inside it.

5   The original **paraphernalia** for the lottery had been lost long ago, and the black box now resting on the stool had been put into use even before Old Man Warner, the oldest man in town, was born. Mr. Summers spoke frequently to the villagers about making a new box, but no one liked to upset even as much **tradition** as was represented by the black box. There was a story that the present box had been made with some pieces of the box that had preceded it, the one that had been constructed when the first people settled down to make a village here. Every year, after the lottery, Mr. Summers began talking again about a new box, but every year the subject was allowed to fade off without anything's being done. The black box grew shabbier each year: by now it was no longer completely black but splintered badly along one side to show the original wood color, and in some places faded or stained.

6   Mr. Martin and his oldest son, Baxter, held the black box securely on the stool until Mr. Summers had stirred the papers thoroughly with his hand. Because so much of the ritual had been forgotten or discarded, Mr. Summers had been successful in having slips of paper substituted for the chips of wood that had been used for generations. Chips of wood, Mr. Summers had argued, had been all very well when the village was tiny, but now that the population was more than three hundred and likely to keep on growing, it was necessary to use something that would fit more easily into he black box. The night before the lottery, Mr. Summers and Mr. Graves made up the slips of paper and put them in the box, and it was then taken to the safe of Mr. Summers' coal company and locked up until Mr. Summers was ready to take it to the

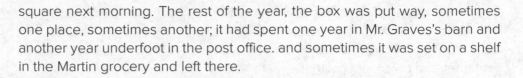

NOTES

square next morning. The rest of the year, the box was put way, sometimes one place, sometimes another; it had spent one year in Mr. Graves's barn and another year underfoot in the post office. and sometimes it was set on a shelf in the Martin grocery and left there.

7   There was a great deal of fussing to be done before Mr. Summers declared the lottery open. There were the lists to make up—of heads of families, heads of households in each family, members of each household in each family. There was the proper swearing-in of Mr. Summers by the postmaster, as the official of the lottery; at one time, some people remembered, there had been a recital of some sort, performed by the official of the lottery, a **perfunctory,** tuneless chant that had been rattled off duly each year; some people believed that the official of the lottery used to stand just so when he said or sang it, others believed that he was supposed to walk among the people, but years and years ago this part of the **ritual** had been allowed to lapse. There had been, also, a ritual salute, which the official of the lottery had had to use in addressing each person who came up to draw from the box, but this also had changed with time, until now it was felt necessary only for the official to speak to each person approaching. Mr. Summers was very good at all this; in his clean white shirt and blue jeans, with one hand resting carelessly on the black box, he seemed very proper and important as he talked interminably to Mr. Graves and the Martins.

8   Just as Mr. Summers finally left off talking and turned to the assembled villagers, Mrs. Hutchinson came hurriedly along the path to the square, her sweater thrown over her shoulders, and slid into place in the back of the crowd. "Clean forgot what day it was," she said to Mrs. Delacroix, who stood next to her, and they both laughed softly. "Thought my old man was out back stacking wood," Mrs. Hutchinson went on, "and then I looked out the window and the kids was gone, and then I remembered it was the twenty-seventh and came a-running." She dried her hands on her apron, and Mrs. Delacroix said, "You're in time, though. They're still talking away up there."

9   Mrs. Hutchinson craned her neck to see through the crowd and found her husband and children standing near the front. She tapped Mrs. Delacroix on the arm as a farewell and began to make her way through the crowd. The people separated good-humoredly to let her through; two or three people said, in voices just loud enough to be heard across the crowd, "Here comes your Missus, Hutchinson," and "Bill, she made it after all." Mrs. Hutchinson reached her husband, and Mr. Summers, who had been waiting, said cheerfully, "Thought we were going to have to get on without you, Tessie." Mrs. Hutchinson said, grinning, "Wouldn't have me leave m'dishes in the sink, now, would you. Joe?" and soft laughter ran through the crowd as the people stirred back into position after Mrs. Hutchinson's arrival.

NOTES

10   "Well, now," Mr. Summers said soberly, "guess we better get started, get this over with, so's we can go back to work. Anybody ain't here?"

11   "Dunbar," several people said. "Dunbar, Dunbar."

12   Mr. Summers consulted his list. "Clyde Dunbar," he said. "That's right. He's broke his leg, hasn't he? Who's drawing for him?"

13   "Me, I guess," a woman said, and Mr. Summers turned to look at her. "Wife draws for her husband," Mr. Summers said. "Don't you have a grown boy to do it for you, Janey?" Although Mr. Summers and everyone else in the village knew the answer perfectly well, it was the business of the official of the lottery to ask such questions formally. Mr. Summers waited with an expression of polite interest while Mrs. Dunbar answered.

14   "Horace's not but sixteen yet," Mrs. Dunbar said regretfully. "Guess I gotta fill in for the old man this year."

15   "Right," Mr. Summers said. He made a note on the list he was holding. Then he asked, "Watson boy drawing this year?"

16   A tall boy in the crowd raised his hand. "Here," he said. "I m drawing for m'mother and me." He blinked his eyes nervously and ducked his head as several voices in the crowd said things like "Good fellow, Jack," and "Glad to see your mother's got a man to do it."

17   "Well," Mr. Summers said, "guess that's everyone. Old Man Warner make it?"

18   "Here," a voice said, and Mr. Summers nodded.

19   A sudden hush fell on the crowd as Mr. Summers cleared his throat and looked at the list. "All ready?" he called. "Now, I'll read the names—heads of families first—and the men come up and take a paper out of the box. Keep the paper folded in your hand without looking at it until everyone has had a turn. Everything clear?"

20   The people had done it so many times that they only half listened to the directions; most of them were quiet, wetting their lips, not looking around. Then Mr. Summers raised one hand high and said, "Adams." A man disengaged himself from the crowd and came forward. "Hi, Steve," Mr. Summers said, and Mr. Adams said, "Hi, Joe." They grinned at one another humorlessly and nervously. Then Mr. Adams reached into the black box and took out a folded paper. He held it firmly by one corner as he turned and went hastily back to his place in the crowd, where he stood a little apart from his family, not looking down at his hand.

Please note that excerpts and passages in the StudySync® library and this workbook are intended as touchstones to generate interest in an author's work. The excerpts and passages do not substitute for the reading of entire texts, and StudySync® strongly recommends that students seek out and purchase the whole literary or informational work in order to experience it as the author intended. Links to online resellers are available in our digital library. In addition, complete works may be ordered through an authorized reseller by filling out and returning to StudySync® the order form enclosed in this workbook.

Reading & Writing Companion   13

21 "Allen," Mr. Summers said. "Anderson. . . . Bentham."

22 "Seems like there's no time at all between lotteries any more," Mrs. Delacroix said to Mrs. Graves in the back row. "Seems like we got through with the last one only last week."

23 "Time sure goes fast," Mrs. Graves said.

24 "Clark. . . . Delacroix."

25 "There goes my old man," Mrs. Delacroix said. She held her breath while her husband went forward.

26 "Dunbar," Mr. Summers said, and Mrs. Dunbar went steadily to the box while one of the women said, "Go on, Janey," and another said, "There she goes."

27 "We're next," Mrs. Graves said. She watched while Mr. Graves came around from the side of the box, greeted Mr. Summers gravely and selected a slip of paper from the box. By now, all through the crowd there were men holding the small folded papers in their large hands, turning them over and over nervously Mrs. Dunbar and her two sons stood together, Mrs. Dunbar holding the slip of paper.

28 "Harburt. . . . Hutchinson."

29 "Get up there, Bill," Mrs. Hutchinson said, and the people near her laughed.

30 "Jones."

31 "They do say," Mr. Adams said to Old Man Warner, who stood next to him, "that over in the north village they're talking of giving up the lottery."

32 Old Man Warner snorted, "Pack of crazy fools," he said. "Listening to the young folks, nothing's good enough for them. Next thing you know, they'll be wanting to go back to living in caves, nobody work any more, live that way for a while. Used to be a saying about 'Lottery in June, corn be heavy soon.' First thing you know, we'd all be eating stewed chickweed and acorns. There's always been a lottery," he added petulantly. "Bad enough to see young Joe Summers up there joking with everybody."

33 "Some places have already quit lotteries," Mrs. Adams said.

34 "Nothing but trouble in that," Old Man Warner said stoutly. "Pack of young fools."

35 "Martin." And Bobby Martin watched his father go forward. "Overdyke. . . . Percy."

36 "I wish they'd hurry," Mrs. Dunbar said to her older son. "I wish they'd hurry."

37 "They're almost through," her son said.

38 "You get ready to run tell Dad," Mrs. Dunbar said.

39 Mr. Summers called his own name and then stepped forward precisely and selected a slip from the box. Then he called, "Warner."

40 "Seventy-seventh year I been in the lottery," Old Man Warner said as he went through the crowd. "Seventy-seventh time."

41 "Watson." The tall boy came awkwardly through the crowd. Someone said, "Don't be nervous, Jack," and Mr. Summers said, "Take your time, son."

42 "Zanini."

43 After that, there was a long pause, a breathless pause, until Mr. Summers, holding his slip of paper in the air, said, "All right, fellows." For a minute, no one moved, and then all the slips of paper were opened. Suddenly, all the women began to speak at once, saying, "Who is it?" "Who's got it?" "Is it the Dunbars?," "Is it the Watsons?" Then the voices began to say, "It's Hutchinson. It's Bill," "Bill Hutchinson's got it."

44 "Go tell your father," Mrs. Dunbar said to her older son.

45 People began to look around to see the Hutchinsons. Bill Hutchinson was standing quiet, staring down at the paper in his hand. Suddenly, Tessie Hutchinson shouted to Mr. Summers, "You didn't give him time enough to take any paper he wanted. I saw you. It wasn't fair!"

46 "Be a good sport, Tessie, " Mrs. Delacroix called, and Mrs. Graves said, "All of us took the same chance."

47 "Shut up, Tessie," Bill Hutchinson said.

48 "Well, everyone," Mr. Summers said, "that was done pretty fast, and now we've got to be hurrying a little more to get done in time." He consulted his next list. "Bill," he said, "you draw for the Hutchinson family. You got any other households in the Hutchinsons?"

49 "There's Don and Eva," Mrs. Hutchinson yelled. "Make them take their chance!"

50 "Daughters draw with their husbands' families, Tessie," Mr. Summers said gently. "You know that as well as anyone else."

51 "It wasn't fair," Tessie said.

52 "I guess not, Joe," Bill Hutchinson said regretfully. "My daughter draws with her husband's family, that's only fair. And I've got no other family except the kids."

53 "Then, as far as drawing for families is concerned, it's you," Mr. Summers said in explanation, "and as far as drawing for households is concerned, that's you, too. Right?"

54 "Right," Bill Hutchinson said.

55 "How many kids, Bill?" Mr. Summers asked formally.

56 "Three," Bill Hutchinson said. "There's Bill, Jr., and Nancy, and little Dave. And Tessie and me."

57 "All right, then," Mr. Summers said. "Harry, you got their tickets back?"

58 Mr. Graves nodded and held up the slips of paper. "Put them in the box, then," Mr. Summers directed. "Take Bill's and put it in."

59 "I think we ought to start over," Mrs. Hutchinson said, as quietly as she could. "I tell you it wasn't fair. You didn't give him time enough to choose. Everybody saw that."

60 Mr. Graves had selected the five slips and put them in the box, and he dropped all the papers but those onto the ground, where the breeze caught them and lifted them off.

61 "Listen, everybody," Mrs. Hutchinson was saying to the people around her.

62 "Ready, Bill?" Mr. Summers asked, and Bill Hutchinson, with one quick glance around at his wife and children, nodded.

63 "Remember," Mr. Summers said, "take the slips and keep them folded until each person has taken one. Harry, you help little Dave." Mr. Graves took the hand of the little boy, who came willingly with him up to the box. "Take a paper out of the box, Davy," Mr. Summers said. Davy put his hand into the box and laughed. "Take just one paper," Mr. Summers said. "Harry, you hold it for him." Mr. Graves took the child's hand and removed the folded paper from the tight fist and held it while little Dave stood next to him and looked up at him wonderingly.

64 "Nancy next," Mr. Summers said. Nancy was twelve, and her school friends breathed heavily as she went forward, switching her skirt, and took a slip daintily from the box "Bill, Jr.," Mr. Summers said, and Billy, his face red and his

feet overlarge, nearly knocked the box over as he got a paper out. "Tessie," Mr. Summers said. She hesitated for a minute, looking around defiantly, and then set her lips and went up to the box. She snatched a paper out and held it behind her.

65   "Bill," Mr. Summers said, and Bill Hutchinson reached into the box and felt around, bringing his hand out at last with the slip of paper in it.

66   The crowd was quiet. A girl whispered, "I hope it's not Nancy," and the sound of the whisper reached the edges of the crowd.

67   "It's not the way it used to be," Old Man Warner said clearly. "People ain't the way they used to be."

68   "All right," Mr. Summers said. "Open the papers. Harry, you open little Dave's."

69   Mr. Graves opened the slip of paper and there was a general sigh through the crowd as he held it up and everyone could see that it was blank. Nancy and Bill. Jr., opened theirs at the same time, and both beamed and laughed, turning around to the crowd and holding their slips of paper above their heads.

70   "Tessie," Mr. Summers said. There was a pause, and then Mr. Summers looked at Bill Hutchinson, and Bill unfolded his paper and showed it. It was blank.

71   "It's Tessie," Mr. Summers said, and his voice was hushed. "Show us her paper. Bill."

72   Bill Hutchinson went over to his wife and forced the slip of paper out of her hand. It had a black spot on it, the black spot Mr. Summers had made the night before with the heavy pencil in the coal company office. Bill Hutchinson held it up, and there was a stir in the crowd.

73   "All right, folks," Mr. Summers said. "Let's finish quickly."

74   Although the villagers had forgotten the ritual and lost the original black box, they still remembered to use stones. The pile of stones the boys had made earlier was ready; there were stones on the ground with the blowing scraps of paper that had come out of the box. Mrs. Delacroix selected a stone so large she had to pick it up with both hands and turned to Mrs. Dunbar. "Come on," she said. "Hurry up."

75   Mrs. Dunbar had small stones in both hands, and she said. gasping for breath, "I can't run at all. You'll have to go ahead and I'll catch up with you."

76   The children had stones already, and someone gave little Davy Hutchinson few pebbles.

NOTES

77 Tessie Hutchinson was in the center of a cleared space by now, and she held her hands out desperately as the villagers moved in on her. "It isn't fair," she said. A stone hit her on the side of the head.

78 Old Man Warner was saying, "Come on, come on, everyone." Steve Adams was in the front of the crowd of villagers, with Mrs. Graves beside him.

79 "It isn't fair, it isn't right," Mrs. Hutchinson screamed and then they were upon her.

"The Lottery" from THE LOTTERY by Shirley Jackson. Copyright © 1948, 1949 by Shirley Jackson. Copyright renewed 1976, 1977 by Laurence Hyman, Barry Hyman, Mrs. Sarah Webster and Mrs. Joanne Schnurer. Reprinted by permission of Farrar, Straus and Giroux, LLC.

THINK QUESTIONS

CA-CCSS: CA.RL.7.1, CA.RL.7.3, CA.L.7.4a, CA.L.7.4c, CA.L.7.4d, CA.L.7.5b, CA.SL.7.1a, CA.SL.7.1c, CA.SL.7.1d, CA.SL.7.2, CA.SL.7.3, CA.SL.7.4

1. What specific details in the first paragraph describe the day on which the lottery takes place? Why do you think the story gives such specific details about the setting—the time and place of the story?

2. How does the lottery affect Tessie Hutchinson and her family at the end of the story? How is this a good example of how plot can influence characters? Cite specific textual evidence to support your statements.

3. What saying does Old Man Warner recite about the lottery, in paragraph 32? What does this tell you about the original reason for holding the lottery? What evidence in the text suggests that Old Man Warner thinks that giving up the lottery would have serious consequences for the townspeople? Cite specific textual evidence to support your statements.

4. Use context clues to determine the meaning of the word **tradition** as it is used in paragraph 5 of "The Lottery." Write your definition of "tradition" and explain how you figured out the meaning.

5. Knowing that the small word "lot" is contained in the word "lottery" can help you figure out the meaning of **lottery.** Use a dictionary to find several meanings for the word "lot," but jot down only those meanings that focus on the idea that something is decided by chance. Use these meanings of "lot" to help you determine the meaning of "lottery." Write your definition of "lottery" and tell how you figured out the meaning. Refer to the dictionary again to confirm or revise your definition.

CLOSE READ

CA-CCSS: CA.RL.7.1, CA.RL.7.2, CA.RL.7.3, CA.W.7.2a, CA.W.7.2b, CA.W.7.2c, CA.W.7.2d, CA.W.7.2e, CA.W.7.2f, CA.W.7.4, CA.W.7.5, CA.W.7.6, CA.W.7.10

Reread the short story "The Lottery." As you reread, complete the Focus Questions below. Then use your answers and annotations from the questions to help you complete the Writing Prompt.

FOCUS QUESTIONS

1. As you reread "The Lottery," remember that the actions of the characters can affect the plot. In paragraph 2, how do the actions of the village boys affect the development of the plot over the course of the text? Highlight evidence in the text and make annotations to explain your answer.

2. In paragraph 4, what can you infer from the hesitation on the part of some of the characters to help with the handling of the black box? Highlight evidence from the text and write annotations to support your inferences.

3. In paragraphs 5–7, what specific evidence from the text supports the idea that the villagers are carrying on a tradition that they no longer fully understand? Highlight textual evidence and make annotations to explain your choices.

4. In paragraph 8, what character does the author introduce who will influence both the plot and the theme? What information about the character becomes ironic as the plot develops? Highlight your evidence and make annotations to explain your thinking.

5. How do Tessie Hutchinson's actions at the end of the story help you understand how character can affect both the plot and the theme? Through the influence of setting, character, and plot, how does the theme of the story get across a message about injustice and unjust societies? Highlight your evidence and make annotations to explain your inferences.

WRITING PROMPT

Sometimes what you expect to happen doesn't happen. That is the case with "The Lottery." Explain how story elements interact in the text to lead to the surprise ending. For example, how did the warm, bright setting interact with the plot to lead you to expect that something good would happen in the story? Use precise language to demonstrate your understanding of story elements. Then provide examples of how characters influenced the plot or the plot influenced characters to turn your expectations upside down and produce the story's shocking ending. Use transitions to clarify relationships between (or among) your examples. Cite specific evidence from the text to support your response. Maintain a formal writing style and end with a strong conclusion.

Please note that excerpts and passages in the StudySync® library and this workbook are intended as touchstones to generate interest in an author's work. The excerpts and passages do not substitute for the reading of entire texts, and StudySync® strongly recommends that students seek out and purchase the whole literary or informational work in order to experience it as the author intended. Links to online resellers are available in our digital library. In addition, complete works may be ordered through an authorized reseller by filling out and returning to StudySync® the order form enclosed in this workbook.

Reading & Writing Companion   19

THE GIVER

FICTION
Lois Lowry
1993

INTRODUCTION

In Jonas's community, there is no hunger, disease, or poverty, but also little individual choice. All major decisions are trusted to the Committee of Elders, and at age twelve, each community member is assigned a career path by the Committee. In this excerpt, Jonas, who will soon turn twelve, expresses his concerns about the future to his parents.

"It was a secret selection, made by the leaders of the community, the Committee of Elders..."

FIRST READ

NOTES

Excerpt from Chapter 2

1   Jonas shivered. He pictured his father, who must have been a shy and quiet boy, for he was a shy and quiet man, seated with his group, waiting to be called to the stage. The Ceremony of Twelve was the last of the Ceremonies. The most important.

2   "I remember how proud my parents looked—and my sister, too; even though she wanted to be out riding the bicycle publicly, she stopped fidgeting and was very still and **attentive** when my turn came.

3   "But to be honest, Jonas," his father said, "for me there was not the element of suspense that there is with your Ceremony. Because I was already fairly certain of what my Assignment was to be."

4   Jonas was surprised. There was no way, really, to know in advance. It was a secret selection, made by the leaders of the community, the Committee of **Elders,** who took the responsibility so seriously that there were never even any jokes made about assignments.

5   His mother seemed surprised, too. "How could you have known?" she asked.

6   His father smiled his gentle smile. "Well, it was clear to me—and my parents later confessed that it had been obvious to them, too—what my **aptitude** was. I had always loved the newchildren more than anything. When my friends in my age group were holding bicycle races, or building toy vehicles or bridges with their construction sets, or—"

7   "All the things I do with my friends," Jonas pointed out, and his mother nodded in agreement.

8   "I always participated, of course, because as children we must experience all of those things. And I studied hard in school, just as you do, Jonas. But again and again, during free time, I found myself drawn to the newchildren. I spent almost all of my volunteer hours helping in the Nurturing Center. Of course the Elders knew that, from their observation."

9   Jonas nodded. During the past year he had been aware of the increasing level of observation. In school, at recreation time, and during volunteer hours, he had noticed the Elders watching him and the other Elevens. He had seen them taking notes. He knew, too, that the Elders were meeting for long hours with all of the instructors that he and the other Elevens had had during their years of school.

10 "So I expected it, and I was pleased, but not at all surprised, when my Assignment was announced as **Nurturer,**" Father explained.

11 "Did everyone applaud, even though they weren't surprised?" Jonas asked.

12 "Oh, of course. They were happy for me, that my Assignment was what I wanted most. I felt very fortunate." His father smiled.

13 "Were any of the Elevens disappointed, your year?" Jonas asked. Unlike his father, he had no idea what his Assignment would be. But he knew that some would disappoint him. Though he respected his father's work, Nurturer would not be his wish. And he didn't **envy** Laborers at all.

14 His father thought. "No, I don't think so. Of course the Elders are so careful in their observations and selections."

15 "I think it's probably the most important job in our community," his mother commented.

16 "My friend Yoshiko was surprised by her selection as Doctor," Father said, "but she was thrilled. And let's see, there was Andrei—I remember that when we were boys he never wanted to do physical things. He spent all the recreation time he could with his construction set, and his volunteer hours were always on building sites. The Elders knew that, of course. Andrei was given the Assignment of Engineer and he was delighted."

17 "Andrei later designed the bridge that crosses the river to the west of town," Jonas's mother said. "It wasn't there when we were children."

18 "There are very rarely disappointments, Jonas. I don't think you need to worry about that," his father reassured him. "And if there are, you know there's an appeal process." But they all laughed at that—an appeal went to a committee for study.

NOTES

19   "I worry a little about Asher's Assignment," Jonas confessed. "Asher's such *fun*. But he doesn't really have any serious interests. He makes a game out of everything."

20   His father chuckled. "You know," he said, "I remember when Asher was a newchild at the Nurturing Center, before he was named. He never cried. He giggled and laughed at everything. All of us on the staff enjoyed nurturing Asher."

21   "The Elders know Asher," his mother said. "They'll find exactly the right Assignment for him. I don't think you need to worry about him. But, Jonas, let me warn you about something that may not have occurred to you. I know I didn't think about it until after my Ceremony of Twelve."

22   "What's that?"

23   "Well, it's the last of the Ceremonies, as you know. After Twelve, age isn't important. Most of us even lose track of how old we are as time passes, though the information is in the Hall of Open Records, and we could go and look it up if we wanted to. What's important is the preparation for adult life, and the training you'll receive in your Assignment."

24   "I know that," Jonas said. "Everyone knows that."

25   "But it means," his mother went on, "that you'll move into a new group. And each of your friends will. You'll no longer be spending your time with your group of Elevens. After the Ceremony of Twelve, you'll be with your Assignment group, with those in training. No more volunteer hours. No more recreation hours. So your friends will no longer be as close."

26   Jonas shook his head. "Asher and I will always be friends," he said firmly. "And there will still be school."

27   "That's true," his father agreed. "But what your mother said is true as well. There will be changes."

28   "*Good* changes, though," his mother pointed out.

Excerpted from The Giver *by Lois Lowry, published by Houghton Mifflin Harcourt.*

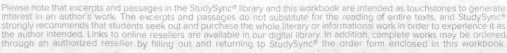

THINK QUESTIONS   CA-CCSS: CA.RL.7.1, CA.L.7.4a, CA.L.7.4c, CA.SL.7.1a, CA.SL.7.1c, CA.SL.7.2, CA.SL.7.3

1. Refer to one or more details in the text to support your understanding of why Jonas "shivered" in the opening line of the excerpt. Cite specific details that are directly stated in the text and inferences you made from clues in the first three paragraphs.

2. Why didn't Jonas's father feel an element of suspense at his Ceremony of Twelve? What is Jonas's reaction to his father's lack of suspense at his Ceremony? Cite textual evidence from paragraphs 3, 4, and 6 to support your response.

3. Use specific evidence from the text to explain why Jonas is concerned about Asher's assignment. Then explain why Jonas's mother is not worried about Asher. What can you infer about Jonas and his mother from their contrasting points of view about Asher in paragraphs 19 and 21?

4. Use context from paragraph 6 to determine the meaning of the word **aptitude** as it is used in *The Giver*. Write your definition of "aptitude" and explain how you determined the meaning of the word. Cite specific evidence from the text.

5. Use a print or digital dictionary to determine the meaning of **elders** as it is used in paragraph 4 of the excerpt. Write the definition. Then provide evidence from the paragraph to confirm that the word is being used correctly in the text.

CLOSE READ

CA-CCSS: CA.RL.7.1, CA.RL.7.6, CA.W.7.2a, CA.W.7.2b, CA.W.7.2c, CA.W.7.2d, CA.W.7.2e, CA.W.7.2f, CA.W.7.4, CA.W.7.5, CA.W.7.6, CA.W.7.10

Reread the excerpt from *The Giver*. As you reread, complete the Focus Questions below. Then use your answers and annotations from the questions to help you complete the Writing Prompt.

FOCUS QUESTIONS

1. How do the first four paragraphs of *The Giver* indicate that the narrator is using a third-person limited omniscient point of view to tell the story? Highlight evidence from the text and make annotations to support your explanation.

2. In paragraphs 8 and 9, what evidence indicates that Jonas and his father share the same point of view about the Elders' use of observation to make the Assignments? Highlight evidence from the text and make annotations to support your response.

3. What point of view does Jonas express in paragraph 13 about the different jobs that might be assigned to him? How does his point of view differ from his father's in paragraph 12? Highlight evidence from the text and make annotations to support your answer.

4. How do Jonas's mother's words to him at the end of paragraph 21 and again in paragraphs 23 and 25 express the consequences of the Ceremony? Support your answer with textual evidence and make annotations to explain your response.

5. In paragraphs 13, 18, 19, and 21, what are the basic differences between Jonas's point of view and his parents' point of view about the Ceremony of Twelve? What inference can you make about whether or not they believe they are living in a just society? Highlight evidence from the text and make annotations to support your inferences and ideas.

WRITING PROMPT

How does the point of view from which *The Giver* is told focus on Jonas's thoughts and feelings about the Ceremony of Twelve? How is Jonas's point of view revealed? How does it differ from his parents' point of view about the ceremony? How do the differences contribute to the tension in the story? State a strong topic sentence for your writing. Use transitions to clarify connections between (or among) your ideas. Organize your essay in a logical way and cite specific evidence from the text to support your writing. Maintain a formal writing style and end with a strong conclusion.

Please note that excerpts and passages in the StudySync® library and this workbook are intended as touchstones to generate interest in an author's work. The excerpts and passages do not substitute for the reading of entire texts, and StudySync® strongly recommends that students seek out and purchase the whole literary or informational work in order to experience it as the author intended. Links to online resellers are available in our digital library. In addition, complete works may be ordered through an authorized reseller by filling out and returning to StudySync® the order form enclosed in this workbook.

Reading & Writing Companion   25

THE WISE OLD WOMAN

FICTION

Yoshiko Uchida
1965

INTRODUCTION

The *Wise Old Woman* is a traditional Japanese folktale retold by Yoshiko Uchida, a Japanese-American author who grew up in California during the Great Depression. As a child, Uchida's parents taught her to appreciate the customs and folktales of their native land, and as a result, Japanese culture is prevalent in Uchida's writing. Through her writing, Uchida expressed the hope that "all children, in whatever country they may live, have the same love of fun and a good story."

"'I have no use for old people in my village,' he said haughtily."

FIRST READ

NOTES

1   Many long years ago, there lived an **arrogant** and cruel young lord who ruled over a small village in the western hills of Japan.

2   "I have no use for old people in my village," he said haughtily. "They are neither useful nor able to work for a living. I therefore **decree** that anyone over seventy-one must be **banished** from the village and left in the mountains to die."

3   "What a dreadful decree! What a cruel and unreasonable lord we have," the people of the village murmured. But the lord fearfully punished anyone who disobeyed him, and so villagers who turned seventy-one were tearfully carried into the mountains, never to return.

4   Gradually there were fewer and fewer old people in the village and soon they disappeared altogether. Then the young lord was pleased.

5   "What a fine village of young, healthy, and hard-working people I have," he bragged. "Soon it will be the finest village in all of Japan."

6   Now, there lived in this village a kind young farmer and his aged mother. They were poor, but the farmer was good to his mother, and the two of them lived happily together. However, as the years went by, the mother grew older, and before long she reached the terrible age of seventy-one.

7   "If only I could some how **deceive** the cruel lord," the farmer thought. But there were records in the village books and everyone knew that his mother had turned seventy-one.

8   Each day the son put off telling his mother that he must take her into the mountains to die, but the people of the village began to talk. The farmer knew

that if he did not take his mother away soon, the lord would send his soldiers and throw them both into a dark dungeon to die a terrible death.

9   "Mother—" he would begin, as he tried to tell her what he must do, but he could not go on.

10 Then one day the mother herself spoke of the lord's dread decree. "Well, my son," she said, "the time has come for you to take me to the mountains. We must hurry before the lord sends his soldiers for you." And she did not seem worried at all that she must go to the mountains to die.

11 "Forgive me, dear mother, for what I must do," the farmer said sadly, and the next morning he lifted his mother to his shoulders and set off on the steep path toward the mountains. Up and up he climbed, until the trees clustered close and the path was gone. There was no longer even the sound of birds, and they heard only the soft wail of the wind in the trees. The son walked slowly, for he could not bear to think of leaving his old mother in the mountains. On and on he climbed, not wanting to stop and leave her behind. Soon, he heard his mother breaking off small twigs from the trees that they passed.

12 "Mother, what are you doing?" he asked.

13 "Do not worry, my son," she answered gently. "I am just marking the way so you will not get lost returning to the village."

14 The son stopped. "Even now you are thinking of me?" he asked, wonderingly.

15 The mother nodded. "Of course, my son," she replied. "You will always be in my thoughts. How could it be otherwise?"

16 At that, the young farmer could bear it no longer. "Mother, I cannot leave you in the mountains to die all alone," he said. "We are going home and no matter what the lord does to punish me, I will never desert you again."

17 So they waited until the sun had set and a lone star crept into the silent sky. Then, in the dark shadows of night, the farmer carried his mother down the hill and they returned quietly to their little house. The farmer dug a deep hole in the floor of his kitchen and made a small room where he could hide his mother. From that day, she spent all her time in the secret room and the farmer carried meals to her there. The rest of the time, he was careful to work in the fields and act as though he lived alone. In this way, for almost two years he kept his mother safely hidden and no one in the village knew that she was there.

18   Then one day there was a terrible **commotion** among the villagers, for Lord Higa of the town beyond the hills threatened to conquer their village and make it his own.

19   "Only one thing can spare you," Lord Higa announced. "Bring me a box containing one thousand ropes of ash and I will spare your village."

20   The cruel young lord quickly gathered together all the wise men of his village. "You are men of wisdom," he said. "Surely you can tell me how to meet Lord Higa's demands so our village can be spared."

21   But the wise men shook their heads. "It is impossible to make even one rope of ash, sire," they answered. "How can we ever make one thousand?"

22   "Fools!" the lord cried angrily. "What good is your wisdom if you cannot help me now?"

23   And he posted a notice in the village square offering a great reward of gold to any villager who could help him save their village.

24   But all the people in the village whispered, "Surely, it is an impossible thing, for ash crumbles at the touch of the finger. How could anyone ever make a rope of ash?" They shook their heads and sighed, "Alas, alas, we must be conquered by yet another cruel lord."

25   The young farmer, too, supposed that this must be, and he wondered what would happen to his mother if a new lord even more terrible than their own came to rule over them.

26   When his mother saw the troubled look on his face, she asked, "Why are you so worried, my son?"

27   So the farmer told her of the impossible demand made by Lord Higa if the village was to be spared, but his mother did not seem troubled at all. Instead she laughed softly and said, "Why, that is not such an impossible task. All one has to do is soak ordinary rope in salt water and dry it well. When it is burned, it will hold its shape and there is your rope of ash! Tell the villagers to hurry and find one thousand pieces of rope."

28   The farmer shook his head in amazement. "Mother, you are wonderfully wise," he said, and he rushed to tell the young lord what he must do.

29   "You are wiser than all the wise men of the village," the lord said when he heard the farmer's solution, and he rewarded him with many pieces of gold. The thousand ropes of ash were quickly made and the village was spared.

30 In a few days, however, there was another great commotion in the village as Lord Higa sent another threat. This time he sent a log with a small hole that curved and bent seven times through its length, and he demanded that a single piece of silk thread be threaded through the hole. "If you cannot perform this task," the lord threatened, "I shall come to conquer your village."

31 The young lord hurried once more to his wise men, but they all shook their heads in bewilderment. "A needle cannot bend its way through such curves," they moaned. "Again we are faced with an impossible demand."

32 "And again you are stupid fools!" the lord said, stamping his foot impatiently. He then posted a second notice in the village square asking the villagers for their help.

33 Once more the young farmer hurried with the problem to his mother in her secret room.

34 "Why, that is not so difficult," his mother said with a quick smile. "Put some sugar at one end of the hole. Then tie an ant to a piece of silk thread and put it in at the other end. He will weave his way in and out of the curves to get to the sugar and he will take the silk thread with him."

35 "Mother, you are remarkable!" the son cried, and he hurried off to the lord with the solution to the second problem.

36 Once more the lord **commended** the young farmer and rewarded him with many pieces of gold. "You are a brilliant man and you have saved our village again," he said gratefully.

37 But the lord's troubles were not over even then, for a few days later Lord Higa sent still another demand. "This time you will undoubtedly fail and then I shall conquer your village," he threatened. "Bring me a drum that sounds without being beaten."

38 "But that is not possible," sighed the people of the village. "How can anyone make a drum sound without beating it?"

39 This time the wise men held their heads in their hands and moaned, "It is hopeless. It is hopeless. This time Lord Higa will conquer us all."

40 The young farmer hurried home breathlessly. "Mother, Mother, we must solve another terrible problem or Lord Higa will conquer our village!" And he quickly told his mother about the impossible drum.

41   His mother, however, smiled and answered, "Why, this is the easiest of them all. Make a drum with sides of paper and put a bumblebee inside. As it tries to escape, it will buzz and beat itself against the paper and you will have a drum that sounds without being beaten."

42   The young farmer was amazed at his mother's wisdom. "You are far wiser than any of the wise men of the village," he said, and he hurried to tell the young lord how to meet Lord Higa's third demand.

43   When the lord heard the answer, he was greatly impressed. "Surely a young man like you cannot be wiser than all my wise men," he said. "Tell me honestly, who has helped you solve all these difficult problems?"

44   The young farmer could not lie. "My lord," he began slowly, "for the past two years I have broken the law of the land. I have kept my aged mother hidden beneath the floor of my house, and it is she who solved each of your problems and saved the village from Lord Higa."

45   He trembled as he spoke, for he feared the lord's displeasure and rage. Surely now the soldiers would be summoned to throw him into the dark dungeon. But when he glanced fearfully at the lord, he saw that the young ruler was not angry at all. Instead, he was silent and thoughtful, for at last he realized how much wisdom and knowledge old people possess.

46   "I have been very wrong," he said finally. "And I must ask the forgiveness of your mother and of all my people. Never again will I demand that the old people of our village be sent to the mountains to die. Rather, they will be treated with the respect and honor they deserve and share with us the wisdom of their years."

47   And so it was. From that day, the villagers were no longer forced to abandon their parents in the mountains, and the village became once more a happy, cheerful place in which to live. The terrible Lord Higa stopped sending his impossible demands and no longer threatened to conquer them, for he too was impressed.

48   "Even in such a small village there is much wisdom," he declared, "and its people should be allowed to live in peace."

49   And that is exactly what the farmer and his mother and all the people of the village did for all the years thereafter.

© 1965 by Yoshiko Uchida, THE SEA OF GOLD AND OTHER TALES FROM JAPAN. Reproduced by permission of The Bancroft Library, on behalf of the Regents of the University of California.

THINK QUESTIONS CA-CCSS: CA.RL.7.1, CA.L.7.4a, CA.L.7.4c

1. Why did the young lord issue a decree against elderly people? What did the decree say? Cite specific evidence from the second paragraph.

2. How does the "old woman" thwart Lord Higa and save the village? What inference can you make about her from her ability to solve Lord Higa's three difficult tasks? Cite evidence from the text in your response.

3. What made the young lord have a change of heart toward the elderly? How might he behave toward them in the future? Use evidence from paragraphs 41–43 to support your answer.

4. Use context clues to determine the meaning of the word **banished** as it is used in sentence 3 of paragraph 2. Write your definition of "banished" and explain how you figured out its meaning. Then check your meaning in a print or an online dictionary.

5. The word **decree** is used as a noun and a verb in paragraphs 2 and 3. Use context clues to determine the part of speech of the word in each of these paragraphs. If needed, use a dictionary to define both the noun and verb form of the word. Write your two definitions, and explain how you figured out the meaning of each use of the word.

CLOSE READ
CA-CCSS: CA.RL.7.1, CA.RL.7.2, CA.RL.7.3, CA.RL.7.6, CA.W.7.2a, CA.W.7.4, CA.W.7.5, CA.W.7.6, CA.W.7.10, CA.L.7.4c, CA.L.7.4d

Reread the folktale "The Wise Old Woman." As you reread, complete the Focus Questions below. Then use your answers and annotations from the questions to help you complete the Writing Prompt.

FOCUS QUESTIONS

1. As you reread "The Wise Old Woman," remember that the story is told from the third-person point of view. Although the narrator provides a few indications of what the young lord is thinking or feeling, readers really know only the thoughts of the young farmer. Highlight evidence in paragraphs 7–9 that reveals the farmer's point of view about the young lord's decree, and make annotations to support your ideas.

2. Plot events can also convey details that suggest the theme. Closely reread paragraphs 18–29 and explain how the details in these paragraphs help you begin to identify the theme (or message) of the folktale. Highlight evidence from the text and make annotations to explain your ideas.

3. Analyzing character traits can also provide readers with details that point to the theme of a story. Reread paragraphs 40–43 and highlight specific evidence that suggests what the farmer's mother is like. Make annotations noting how the character traits of the "wise old woman" might play a part in developing the central theme.

4. Which lines from paragraph 46 provide the best evidence of the central theme in this folktale? Highlight the two most important sentences and annotate how they express the theme.

5. In paragraph 7, the young farmer admits that he wishes he could "deceive the cruel lord" and save his aged mother from his terrible decree. What plan does he come up with to save her and in turn all the elderly people in the village? How does his rebellion against the decree, expressed in paragraphs 16–17, suggest his point of view about the society and its ruler? Highlight textual evidence and make annotations about your inferences to support your answer.

WRITING PROMPT

How does the theme of "The Wise Old Woman" help you understand a larger lesson about life, human nature, or the experience of a specific people and culture? Use the details you have compiled from examining the point of view, setting, conflict, and plot, as well as the characters' thoughts, dialogue, feelings, and actions, to:

- write an objective summary of the folktale
- identify the theme
- show how the theme is developed over the course of the text

Remember to support your writing with evidence and inferences from the text. Review the vocabulary words you have learned. Be sure to check each word's etymology, or historical development, in a print or an online dictionary. Make sure that you are using the vocabulary in correct context to its meaning. Be aware of words with multiple meanings and use them appropriately.

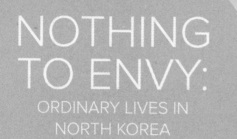

NOTHING TO ENVY:
ORDINARY LIVES IN NORTH KOREA

NON-FICTION
Barbara Demick
2010

INTRODUCTION

I n *Nothing to Envy*, Barbara Demick penetrates the shadowy dictatorship of modern North Korea, focusing on six individuals. The following excerpt features two of the main characters: Mrs. Song, a bookkeeper and loyal supporter of Kim Il-sung's regime, and her daughter Oak-hee, who is dangerously inclined to be skeptical. The episode begins with Mrs. Song and her husband Chang-bo, an independent thinker, watching television, an activity they proudly share with apartment house neighbors who cannot afford the luxury of TV.

"Spying on one's countrymen is something of a national pastime."

FIRST READ

From Chapter Three: The True Believer

1 The program that got Chang-bo in trouble was an innocuous business report about a shoe factory producing rubber boots for the rainy season. The camera panned over crisply efficient workers on an assembly line where the boots were being produced by the thousands. The narrator raved about the superb quality of the boots and reeled off the impressive production statistics.

2 "Hah. If there are so many boots, how come my children never got any?" Chang-bo laughed aloud. The words tumbled out of his mouth before he could consider the consequences.

3 Mrs. Song never figured out which neighbor blabbed. Her husband's remark was quickly reported to the head of the *inminban,* the neighborhood watchdogs, who in turn passed on the information to the Ministry for the Protection of State Security. This ominously named agency is effectively North Korea's political police. It runs an extensive network of informers. By the accounts of defectors, there is at least one informer for every fifty people—more even than East Germany's notorious Stasi, whose files were pried open after German reunification.

4 Spying on one's countrymen is something of a national pastime. There were the young **vigilantes** from the Socialist Youth League like the one who stopped Mrs. Song for not wearing a badge. They also made sure people weren't violating the dress code by wearing blue jeans or T-shirts with Roman writing—considered a capitalist indulgence—or wearing their hair too long. The party issued regular edicts saying that men shouldn't allow the hair on top of their head to grow longer than five centimeters—though an exemption was granted for balding men, who were permitted seven centimeters. If a violation was severe, the offender could be arrested by the Public Standards Police. There were also *kyuch'aldae,* mobile police units who roamed the

streets looking for offenders and had the right to barge into people's houses without notice. They would look for people who used more than their quota of electricity, a light bulb brighter than 40 watts, a hot plate, or a rice cooker. During one of the surprise inspections, one of the neighbors tried to hide their hot plate under a blanket and ended up setting their apartment on fire. The mobile police often dropped in after midnight to see if there were any overnight guests who might have come to visit without travel permits. It was a serious offense, even if it was just an out-of-town relative, and much worse if the guest happened to be a lover. But it wasn't just the police and the volunteer leagues who did the snooping. Everybody was supposed to be vigilant for subversive behavior and transgressions of the rules. Since the country was too poor and the power supply too unreliable for electronic **surveillance,** state security relied on human intelligence—snitches. The newspapers would occasionally run feature stories about heroic children who ratted out their parents. To be denounced by a neighbor for bad-mouthing the regime was nothing extraordinary.

5 Chang-bo's **interrogation** lasted three days. The agents yelled and cursed at him, although they never beat him—at least that's what he told his wife. He claimed afterward that his gift with language helped him talk his way out of the bind. He cited the truth in his defense.

6 "I wasn't insulting anybody. I was simply saying that I haven't been able to buy those boots and I'd like to have some for my family," Chang-bo protested indignantly.

7 He made a convincing case. He was a commanding figure with his potbelly and his stern expression. He looked like the epitome of a Workers' Party official. The political police in the end decided not to push the case and released him without charges.

8 When he returned home, he got a tongue-lashing from his wife that was almost harsher than the interrogation. It was the worst fight of their marriage. For Mrs. Song, it was not merely that her husband had been disrespectful of the government; for the first time in her life, she felt the stirrings of fear. Her conduct had always been so impeccable and her devotion so genuine that it never occurred to her that she might be vulnerable.

9 "Why did you say such nonsense when there were neighbors in the apartment? Didn't you realize you could have jeopardized everything we have?" she railed at him.

10 In fact, they both realized how lucky they were. If not for Chang-bo's excellent class background and his party membership, he would not have been let off so lightly. It helped, too, that Mrs. Song had at various times been head of the *inminban* in the building and commanded some respect from the state

security officers. Chang-bo's offhand remark was precisely the kind of thing that could result in deportation to a prison camp in the mountains if the offender didn't have a solid position in the community. They had heard of a man who cracked a joke about Kim Jong-il's height and was sent away for life. Mrs. Song personally knew a woman from her factory who was taken away for something she wrote in her diary. At the time, Mrs. Song hadn't felt any pity for the woman. "The traitor probably deserved what she got," she'd said to herself. Now she felt embarrassed for having thought such a thing.

11 The incident seemed to blow over. Chastened by the experience, Chang-bo was more careful about what he said outside the family, but his thoughts were running wild. For many years, Chang-bo had been fighting off the doubts that would periodically creep into his consciousness. Now those doubts were gelling into outright disbelief. As a journalist, Chang-bo had more access to information than ordinary people. At the North Hamgyong Provincial Broadcasting Company, where he worked, he and his colleagues heard **uncensored** news reports from the foreign media. It was their job to sanitize it for domestic consumption. Anything positive that happened in capitalist countries or especially South Korea, which in 1988 hosted the Summer Olympics, was downplayed. Strikes, disasters, riots, murders—elsewhere—got plenty of coverage.

12 Chang-bo's job was to report business stories. He toured collective farms, shops, and factories with a notebook and tape recorder, interviewing the managers. Back in the newsroom, he would write his stories in fountain pen (there were no typewriters) about how well the economy was doing. He always put a positive spin on the facts, although he tried to keep them at least plausible. By the time they were edited by his superiors in Pyongyang, however, any glimmer of the truth was gone. Chang-bo knew better than anyone that the supposed triumphs of the North Korean economy were **fabrications.** He had good reason to scoff at the report about the rubber boots.

13 He had one trusted friend from the radio station who shared his increasing disdain for the regime. When the two of them got together, Chang-bo would open a bottle of Mrs. Song's *neungju* and, after a few drinks, they would let rip their true feelings.

14 "What a bunch of liars!" Chang-bo would say in an emphatic tone, taking care just the same not to speak loudly enough for the sound to carry through the thin plaster walls between the apartments.

15 "Crooks, all of them."

16 "The son is even worse than the father."

NOTES

17   Oak-hee eavesdropped on her father and his friend. She nodded quietly in agreement. When her father noticed, he at first tried to shoo her away. Eventually he gave up. Swearing her to secrecy, he took her into his confidence. He told her that Kim Il-sung was not the anti-Japanese resistance fighter he claimed to be so much as a puppet of the Soviet Union. He told her that South Korea was now among the richest countries in Asia; even ordinary working people owned their own cars. Communism, he reported, was proving a failure as an economic system. China and the Soviet Union were now embracing capitalism. Father and daughter would talk for hours, always taking care to keep their voices at a whisper in case a neighbor was snooping around. And, at such times, they always made sure that Mrs. Song, the true believer, was not at home.

Excerpted from *Nothing to Envy: Ordinary Lives in North Korea* by Barbara Demick, published by Spiegel & Grau.

 ## THINK QUESTIONS   CA-CCSS: CA.RI.7.1, CA.L.7.4a, CA.L.7.4b

1. What caused Chang-bo to get into trouble with the Ministry for the Protection of State Security? Cite specific evidence from paragraphs 1–3 to support your response.

2. What helped Chang-bo get off so lightly when he was interrogated? Cite textual evidence from paragraphs 5, 7, and 10.

3. In paragraph 11, the author says that Chang-bo had been fighting off doubts about the North Korean government for many years but that recently "those doubts were gelling into outright disbelief." What textual evidence in paragraphs 11–17 supports this view? How did Chang-bo's job contribute to his disbelief?

4. What is the meaning of **vigilantes** as it is used in paragraph 4 of *Nothing to Envy*? Use context clues to determine the meaning of the word. Write your definition of "vigilantes" and cite the context clues you used to determine its meaning.

5. What is the meaning of **fabrications** as it is used in paragraph 12? Use context clues provided in the paragraph to determine the meaning of the word. Write your definition of "fabrications," and explain how you figured out its meaning. Then check a print or an online dictionary to confirm the meaning.

CLOSE READ

CA-CCSS: CA.RI.7.1, CA.RI.7.3, CA.RI.7.4, CA.L.7.4a, CA.L.7.5, CA.L.7.5a, CA.W.7.2a, CA.W.7.2b, CA.W.7.2c, CA.W.7.2d, CA.W.7.2e, CA.W.7.2f, CA.W.7.4, CA.W.7.5, CA.W.7.6, CA.W.7.10

Reread the excerpt from *Nothing to Envy.* As you reread, complete the Focus Questions below. Then use your answers and annotations from the questions to help you complete the Writing Prompt.

FOCUS QUESTIONS

1. Highlight the idiom "reeled off" in the last sentence of paragraph 1, and make annotations noting the context clues that helped you determine its meaning. Then write a definition of the idiom as it is used in the text.

2. As you reread *Nothing to Envy: Ordinary Lives in North Korea,* look for interactions among ideas, individuals, and events to gain a deeper understanding of the text. For example, in paragraph 4, how did the North Korean economy affect how the government collected information about people? How did the people respond? What terrible events did these people cause? Highlight specific evidence in the text and make annotations to explain your thinking.

3. According to paragraphs 8–10, how did the events surrounding Chang-bo's experience with the state security agents begin to change his wife's ideas about the government? Highlight specific evidence from the text and make annotations to support any inferences you make.

4. In paragraph 13, what does the idiom "let rip" mean? What context clues in paragraphs 13–14 helped you understand the meaning of this idiom as it is used in the text? How does the use of such idioms affect the meaning and tone of the text? Highlight the context clues and make annotations to explain your responses.

5. As you reread the last paragraph, determine to what degree Chang-bo shaped his daughter's ideas. How do you think his daughter feels about living in this society? Draw inferences from the text and highlight the evidence you used to make these inferences. Make annotations to explain your thinking.

WRITING PROMPT

How do ideas influence individuals or events in the text? Choose one important idea or individual, such as Chang-bo, in *Nothing to Envy: Ordinary Lives in North Korea,* and demonstrate how an idea influenced him or her, setting off a chain reaction of events. Introduce your idea with clear and precise language and with vocabulary or idioms from the selection. Use your understanding of informational text elements to determine how ideas, individuals, and events interact in the text. Provide transitions to clarify connections in your information. Use a formal style and cite specific textual evidence to support your response. Complete your writing with an effective conclusion that leaves your audience with an understanding of your topic and with an idea, fact, or question to think about.

FEED

FICTION
M.T. Anderson
2002

INTRODUCTION

.T. Anderson's *Feed* is a young-adult science-fiction novel about a futuristic world in which technology is so intertwined with human life that a computer network feed is implanted directly into people's brains. Here, the narrator of the novel, a teenager named Titus, visits his girlfriend Violet in the hospital, where she is suffering from a malfunction of her feed.

"It's not you," I argued. "It's the feed thing. You're not like that."

FIRST READ

From Part 4: Slumberland

1   87.3%

2   Violet's father got there half an hour after I did. I saw him running past me. I didn't wave or anything, because I didn't want to get in the way or be a pain in the butt. People, sometimes, they need to be alone. He went past me and didn't see who I was. That was okay with me. They took him into the room. I waited.

3   I clapped my hands together softly a bunch of times. I swung my arms at my sides and then clapped. I realized that they were swinging really wide. People were looking up at me. I stopped. I couldn't help a small clap, one last one.

4   He came out. He was walking real slow. He sat down.

5   I didn't know whether to talk to him. He was smoothing out the knees of his tribe-suit.

6   I went over. I said hello, and introduced myself again.

7   He said, "Oh, yes. Hello. Thank you for . . . " He was just like, nodding.

8   "Is she okay?" I asked.

9   "Yes," he said. "Yes. 'Okay.' Yes, she's 'okay.'"

10   He didn't seem much like before.

11   I was like, "What's happening?"

12 "They're fixing the **malfunction**. For the time being. The doctor's coming out." His eyes were orange with the light from his **feed** glasses.

13 The orbs went past. We waited. Two nurses were talking about the weekend. There was nothing I wanted to watch on the feed. It made me feel tired.

14 "Can you stop?" said her father to me.

15 I realized I'd like been clapping again.

16 "I hate rhythms," he said.

17 I put my hands down. I stood still, in front of him.

18 He said, "You can monitor her feed function." He sent me an address. "Go there," he said. "If things **neural** were going swimmingly with Vi, the number you detect would be about ninety-eight percent."

19 I went there. It was some kind of medical site. It said *Violet Durn, Feed Efficiency: 87.3%.* He stared at me. I stared at him. We were like, just, there. The efficiency went up to 87.4%. He turned his head. Someone was whistling two notes in the hallway.

20   ...

21 87.1%

22 The next day, I was at her house. It was all weird. We didn't talk. I don't know why. We didn't open our mouths. We just sat there, silent, chatting.

23 *It's not you,* I argued. *It's the feed thing. You're not like that.*

24 *Maybe I am like that. Maybe that's what's wrong.*

25 She rubbed her hands together. *I'm sorry. Please tell Quendy I'm sorry.*

26 Her father was walking down the stairs near us. We could hear him through the wall.

27 I didn't understand, first. *What?*

28 *I lost a year. During the* seizure. *I can't remember anything from the year before I got the feed. When I was six. The information is just gone. There's nothing there.*

29   She was pressing her palms into her thighs as hard as she could. She watched herself real careful like it was a crafts project. She went, *Nothing. No smells. No talking. No pictures. For a whole year. All gone.*

30   I just looked at her face. There were lines on it I hadn't seen before. She looked sick, like her mouth would taste like the hospital. She saw me looking at her.

31   She was like, *Don't worry, Titus. We're still together. No matter what, we'll still be together.*

32   *Oh,* I went. *Yeah.*

33   She reached out and rubbed my hand. *I'll remember you. I'll hold on to you.*

34   *Oh,* I chatted. *Okay.*

35   She went, . . . *there's so much I need to do. . . . You can't even know. I want to go out right now and start. I want to dance. You know? That's . . . .so cliché, but that's what I see myself doing. I want to dance with like a whole lacrosse team, maybe with them holding me up on a Formica tabletop. I can't even tell you. I want to do the things that show you're alive. . . .*

36   *I want to go on rides. The flume, the teacups, the Tilt-a-Whirl? You know, a big bunch of us on the teacups, with you and me crushed together from the centrifugal force.*

37   I wasn't really wanting to think about us crushed together right then, or about us in a big group, where she might go insane again, so I just looked like, *Yeah. The teacups!*

38   And she was still saying, *I want to see things grazing through field glasses. I want to go someplace now. I want to get . . . out of here and visit some Mayan temples. I want you to take my picture next to the **sacrificial** stone. You know? I want to run down to the beach, I mean, a beach where you can go in the water. I want to have a splashing fight.*

39   I just sat there. Her father was working on something in the basement. It sounded like he had some power tools. Maybe he was drilling, or like, cutting or boring.

40   She went, *They're all sitcom openers.*

41   *What?*

42   *Everything I think of when I think of really living, living to the full—all my ideas are just the opening credits of sitcoms. See what I mean? My idea of life, it's*

Copyright © BookheadEd Learning, LLC

NOTES

what happens when they're rolling the credits. . . . What am I, without the feed? It's all from the feed credits. My idea of real life. You know? Oh, you and I share a snow cone at the park. Oh, funny, it's dribbling down your chin. I wipe it off with my elbow. "Also starring Lurna Ginty as Violet." Oh, happy day! Now we go jump in the fountain! We come out of the tunnel of love! We run through the merry-go-round. You're checking the park with a metal detector! I'm checking the park with a Geiger counter! We wave to the camera!

43 *Except the Mayan ruin.*

44 *What about it?*

45 *There aren't*, I like pointed out, *there aren't the sacrificial stones. In sitcoms.*

46 *No,* she said. *That's right. Chalk one up for the home team.*

47 We sat. She fixed her hair with her hand.

48 I asked her, *What did it feel like. At the party?*

49 She waited. Then, she admitted, *It felt good. Really good, just to scream finally. I felt like I was singing a hit single. . . .*

FEED. Copyright © 2002 by M.T. Anderson. Reproduced by permission of the publisher, Candlewick Press, Somerville, MA.

THINK QUESTIONS CA-CCSS: CA.RL.7.1, CA.L.7.4a, CA.L.7.4b

1. What has happened to Violet? Use evidence from the text that is directly stated or that you have inferred from clues to explain Violet's "illness."

2. What method are Titus and Violet using to chat in paragraph 22? Draw an inference from specific evidence in the text. Support your answer by identifying the textual evidence you used to make your inference.

3. What happened to Violet's memory when she had her seizure? Cite specific textual evidence from paragraph 22 to support your answer.

4. Remembering that the Latin prefix *mal-* means "bad," use the context clues provided in paragraph 12 of the first chapter presented to determine the meaning of **malfunction.** Write your definition of "malfunction" and explain how you determined its meaning.

5. Use context clues to determine the meaning of **feed** as it is used in paragraph 28. Write your definition of "feed" and explain how you figured out the meaning. Be sure to use a print or an online dictionary to confirm your definition.

CLOSE READ   CA-CCSS: CA.RL.7.1, CA.RL.7.6, CA.W.7.2a, CA.W.7.2b, CA.W.7.2c, CA.W.7.2d, CA.W.7.2e, CA.W.7.2f, CA.W.7.4, CA.W.7.5, CA.W.7.6, CA.W.7.10

Reread the excerpt from *Feed*. As you reread, complete the Focus Questions below. Then use your answers and annotations from the questions to help you complete the Writing Prompt.

FOCUS QUESTIONS

1. As you reread *Feed,* highlight specific textual evidence in paragraphs 22–25 that helps you make an inference about what Titus and Violet are "chatting" about. Make annotations about your inference.

2. In paragraphs 28 and 29, Violet doesn't actually say how she feels about losing her memory the year before she got her feed. Highlight specific evidence from the text that helps you draw an inference about how she feels. Make annotations to support your inference.

3. In paragraphs 30–34, Violet's and Titus's points of view about their relationship seem to differ. What inference can you draw from the text to support the idea that they don't view their relationship in the same way? Highlight several pieces of textual evidence and make annotations to support your inference.

4. In paragraphs 35 and 36, Violet expresses that she wants *"to dance with the whole lacrosse team,"* and *"go on rides."* Highlight the specific textual evidence that indicates why she wants to do these things. Make annotations explaining your inferences about her health, based on the evidence.

5. Reread paragraph 42 and highlight the specific textual evidence that allows you to infer that Violet is becoming aware of the unjust society in which she lives. Highlight textual evidence and make annotations to support your inference.

WRITING PROMPT

In a clear thesis statement, make three inferences about what has happened to Violet and how it has influenced her point of view about the society in which she lives. Organize your writing and use textual evidence, such as dialogue, description, and events, to support your inferences, or logical guesses, about what may not be directly stated by the author in the text. Use precise language and transitions to show the connections between (or among) your ideas. Consider your own experiences. What influences your point of view about society? Your answer to this question will lead you to a better understanding of what might affect Violet's point of view. Establish a formal style of writing and end with a strong conclusion to summarize your ideas.

THE HUNGER GAMES

FICTION
Suzanne Collins
2008

INTRODUCTION

Suzanne Collins's dystopian novel, *The Hunger Games*, is set in Panem—what remains of post-apocalyptic North America. In punishment for a failed uprising, the government annually requires each of the twelve districts of Panem to choose one boy and one girl to go to the Capitol, where they must participate in a televised battle to the death. At the selection ceremony, or reaping, for District 12, sixteen-year-old Katniss watches in horror as her little sister, Prim, is chosen for this year's Hunger Games—then rushes to take her place.

"'I volunteer!' I gasp. 'I volunteer as tribute!'"

 FIRST READ

From Chapter 1

1   "You look beautiful," says Prim in a hushed voice.

2   "And nothing like myself," I say. I hug her, because I know these next few hours will be terrible for her. Her first reaping. She's about as safe as you can get, since she's only entered once. I wouldn't let her take out any **tesserae.** But she's worried about me. That the unthinkable might happen.

3   I protect Prim in every way I can, but I'm powerless against the reaping. The anguish I always feel when she's in pain wells up in my chest and threatens to register on my face. I notice her blouse has pulled out of her skirt in the back again and force myself to stay calm. "Tuck your tail in, little duck," I say, smoothing the blouse back in place.

4   Prim giggles and gives me a small "Quack."

5   "Quack yourself," I say with a light laugh. The kind only Prim can draw out of me. "Come on, let's eat," I say and plant a quick kiss on the top of her head.

· · ·

6   It's too bad, really, that they hold the reaping in the square — one of the few places in District 12 that can be pleasant. The square's surrounded by shops, and on public market days, especially if there's good weather, it has a holiday feel to it. But today, despite the bright banners hanging on the buildings, there's an air of grimness. The camera crews, perched like buzzards on rooftops, only add to the effect.

7   People file in silently and sign in. The reaping is a good opportunity for the Capitol to keep tabs on the population as well. Twelve- through eighteen-year-olds are herded into roped areas marked off by ages, the oldest in the

front, the young ones, like Prim, toward the back. Family members line up around the perimeter, holding tightly to one another's hands. But there are others, too, who have no one they love at stake, or who no longer care, who slip among the crowd, taking bets on the two kids whose names will be drawn. **Odds** are given on their ages, whether they're Seam or merchant, if they will break down and weep. Most refuse dealing with the racketeers but carefully, carefully. These same people tend to be informers, and who hasn't broken the law? I could be shot on a daily basis for hunting, but the appetites of those in charge protect me. Not everyone can claim the same.

. . .

8   Just as the town clock strikes two, the mayor steps up to the podium and begins to read. It's the same story every year. He tells of the history of Panem, the country that rose up out of the ashes of a place that was once called North America. He lists the disasters, the droughts, the storms, the fires, the **encroaching** seas that swallowed up so much of the land, the brutal war for what little **sustenance** remained. The result was Panem, a shining Capitol ringed by thirteen districts, which brought peace and prosperity to its citizens. Then came the Dark Days, the uprising of the districts against the Capitol. Twelve were defeated, the thirteenth **obliterated.** The Treaty of Treason gave us the new laws to guarantee peace and, as our yearly reminder that the Dark Days must never be repeated, it gave us the Hunger Games.

9   The rules of the Hunger Games are simple. In punishment for the uprising, each of the twelve districts must provide one girl and one boy, called tributes, to participate. The twenty-four tributes will be imprisoned in a vast outdoor arena that could hold anything from a burning desert to a frozen wasteland. Over a period of several weeks, the competitors must fight to the death. The last tribute standing wins.

10   Taking the kids from our districts, forcing them to kill one another while we watch — this is the Capitol's way of reminding us how totally we are at their mercy. How little chance we would stand of surviving another rebellion.

. . .

11   It's time for the drawing. Effie Trinket says as she always does, "Ladies first!" and crosses to the glass ball with the girls' names. She reaches in, digs her hand deep into the ball, and pulls out a slip of paper. The crowd draws in a collective breath and then you can hear a pin drop, and I'm feeling nauseous and so desperately hoping that it's not me, that it's not me, that it's not me.

12   Effie Trinket crosses back to the podium, smoothes the slip of paper, and reads out the name in a clear voice. And it's not me.

13   It's Primrose Everdeen.

From Chapter 2

14   There must have been some mistake. This can't be happening. Prim was one slip of paper in thousands! Her chances of being chosen were so remote that I'd not even bothered worrying about her. Hadn't I done everything? Taken the tesserae, refused to let her do the same? One slip. One slip in thousands. The odds had been entirely in her favor. But it hadn't mattered.

15   Somewhere far away, I can hear the crowd murmuring unhappily as they always do when a twelve-year-old gets chosen because no one thinks this is fair. And then I see her, the blood drained from her face, hands clenched in fists at her sides, walking with stiff, small steps up toward the stage, passing me, and I see the back of her blouse has become untucked and hangs out over her skirt. It's this detail, the untucked blouse forming a ducktail, that brings me back to myself.

16   "Prim!" The strangled cry comes out of my throat, and my muscles begin to move again. "Prim!" I don't need to shove through the crowd. The other kids make way immediately allowing me a straight path to the stage. I reach her just as she is about to mount the steps. With one sweep of my arm, I push her behind me.

17   "I volunteer!" I gasp. "I volunteer as tribute!"

Excerpted from The Hunger Games *by Suzanne Collins, published by Scholastic Inc.*

THINK QUESTIONS   <small>CA-CCSS: CA.RL.7.1, CA.L.7.4a, CA.L.7.4c, CA.L.7.4d, CA.SL.7.1a, CA.SL.7.1d, CA.SL.7.2, CA.SL.7.3, CA.SL.7.4, CA.SL.7.5, CA.SL.7.6</small>

1. Refer to details in paragraphs 1 and 7 to make inferences about what the reaping is and why Katniss thinks Prim is safe from it.

2. What events led to the Hunger Games, and what purpose are the games meant to serve? Cite specific textual evidence from paragraph 8 to support your answer.

3. In Chapter 2, why is Katniss surprised when Prim is chosen as tribute? What does she do in response? Cite specific evidence from the text to support your response.

4. In *The Hunger Games,* people can purchase **tesserae** by agreeing to enter additional slips in the reaping. The tesserae can then be exchanged for a year's supply of grain or oil. "Tesserae" is a real word with historical roots. Use a print or an online dictionary to find which definition of tesserae most closely matches the way in which the word is used in *The Hunger Games*. Write your definition. Explain how you decided on your choice of meaning.

5. Use context clues to figure out the meaning of the word **sustenance** as it is used in paragraph 8. Write your definition of sustenance and explain how you figured out the meaning. Then use a print or an online dictionary to confirm or revise your definition.

CLOSE READ
CA-CCSS: CA.RL.7.1, CA.RL.7.3, CA.RL.7.7, CA.W.7.2a, CA.W.7.2b, CA.W.7.2c, CA.W.7.2d, CA.W.7.2e, CA.W.7.2f, CA.W.7.4, CA.W.7.5, CA.W.7.6, CA.W.7.10, CA.L.7.4c, CA.L.7.4d

Reread the excerpt from *The Hunger Games*. As you reread, complete the Focus Questions below. Then use your answers and annotations from the questions to help you complete the Writing Prompt.

FOCUS QUESTIONS

1. In order to compare and contrast the text with the film version of *The Hunger Games,* ask your teacher to help you access a video clip on the Web from the feature film. Then view the first 16 seconds of the video clip. Compare it to the details given in paragraph 7 of Chapter 1. Which details from the paragraph are also in the video clip? Which details aren't? Highlight the evidence in the printed text that is also in the video clip of the film, and make annotations to support your answer.

2. Reread paragraphs 11–13 in the text and view the next part of the video clip (up to 0:48). Compare and contrast how the writer builds tension in this part of the plot with the way that the filmmakers do. Highlight specific evidence from the printed text and make annotations to support your comparison.

3. The text in paragraph 14 is not evident in the film. Reread the paragraph and explain why the filmmakers likely chose not to include the narration in the paragraph as dialogue in the scene. How does the film convey Katniss's feelings about what has just happened?

4. Reread paragraph 15 and view the video clip from 0:49 to 1:23. Contrast how the plot details are presented in the printed text and film versions. Why do you think the movie conveys these events in a different way? Highlight evidence in the text and make annotations recording the differences in presentation.

5. Reread paragraphs 16 and 17 and compare the dialogue, characters, and action in the text to the corresponding shot in the video clip (1:24 to 1:34). Then access the audio version of this part of the text (6:18 to 6:44). How do the audio and film versions help you better understand the meaning of "the strangled cry comes out of my throat, and my muscles begin to move again"? How do both of these media help you empathize with Katniss and feel her pain about this unjust society? Cite textual evidence and make annotations to support your answer.

WRITING PROMPT

Consider the three versions of *The Hunger Games*—text, audio, and film—you have analyzed. Think about the similarities and differences in the way the story elements—character, setting, plot, conflict, and narration (or point of view) —are conveyed in each. Also, think about the possible theme that has begun to emerge from the part of the story you have read, heard, and seen. In a clear thesis statement, choose the medium you think would best convey the theme, and provide sound reasons for your choice. Organize and support your writing with relevant evidence from the text, audio, and film, using transitions to clarify relationships among the media. Review the vocabulary words you have learned. Be sure to check each word's etymology, or origin, in a print or digital dictionary. Make sure you are using the vocabulary correctly in context. Be aware of words with multiple meanings and use them appropriately. Use transitions to clarify how your ideas are related. Use a formal writing style and provide a strong conclusion that supports your ideas.

INTRODUCTION

Providing multiple contexts for understanding and interpreting the
Constitution, author Linda Monk explores the history and rationale behind
the seminal text, including its 27 amendments. This excerpt begins as the
constitution itself begins, with a phrase that defines the scope of the entire text,
and the nature of our country as a whole, "We the People." Monk proceeds from
there, line by line, phrase by phrase, to draw a closer focus on the intentions and
meanings of "the words we live by."

"We the People..."

 FIRST READ

From the Preamble

1   "We the People. . ."

2   The first three words of the Constitution are the most important. They clearly state that the people—not the king, not the legislature, not the courts—are the true rulers in American government. This principle is known as popular sovereignty.

3   But who are "We the People"? This question troubled the nation for centuries. As Lucy Stone, one of America's first advocates for women's rights, asked in 1853: "'We the People'? Which 'We the People'? The women were not included." Neither were white males who did not own property, American Indians, or African Americans—slave or free. Justice Thurgood Marshall, the first African American on the Supreme Court, described the limitation:

4   *For a sense of the* **evolving** *nature of the Constitution, we need look no further than the first three words of the document's preamble: 'We the People.' When the founding fathers used this phrase in 1787, they did not have in mind the majority of America's citizens . . . The men who gathered in Philadelphia in 1787 could not . . . have imagined, nor would they have accepted, that the document they were drafting would one day be construed by a Supreme Court to which had been appointed a woman and the descendant of an African slave.*

5   Through the **amendment** process, more and more Americans were eventually included in the Constitution's definition of "We the People." After the Civil War, the Thirteenth Amendment ended slavery, the Fourteenth Amendment gave African Americans citizenship, and the Fifteenth Amendment gave black men the vote. In 1920, the Nineteenth Amendment gave women the right to vote

nationwide, and in 1971, the Twenty-sixth Amendment extended suffrage to eighteen-year-olds.

6   ". . .of the United States, . . ."

7   Like most documents, the Constitution needed a good editor. That person was Gouverneur Morris, who served on the Constitutional Convention's Committee of Style. Morris was the Constitution's chief draftsman, while James Madison was the chief architect. Morris's task was to shape the verbiage of committees into ringing prose. He commented on his work years later: "Having rejected redundant and equivocal terms, I believed it to be as clear as our language would permit."

8   In the Constitution's Preamble, Morris's phrasing had substantive as well as stylistic consequences. The original draft of the Preamble referred to all thirteen states. But, in part because no one knew exactly which states would become the nine required to ratify the Constitution, Morris **condensed** the Preamble into the familiar words of today: "We the People of the United States."

9   Even after the Constitution's ratification, the United States was still evolving from a loose confederation of states into a cohesive national union. Only the Civil War finally achieved the latter. As historian Shelby Foote noted: "Before the war, it was said, 'The United States are.' . . . After the war, it was always 'the United States is.' . . . And that sums up what the war accomplished. It made us an 'is.'"

. . .

10 ". . .this Constitution for the United States of America."

11 The U.S. Constitution is the oldest written constitution of a nation still being used. From the beginning, Americans and others have disagreed about its relative merits. Federalists believed that, by creating a stronger national government, the Constitution would enable the United States to survive among the competing powers of Europe and provide a surer safeguard for liberty at home. Antifederalists feared that the new Constitution would create a new form of tyranny, especially since it lacked a bill of rights. Only by promising that the new Congress would make passage of a bill of rights its top priority did the Federalists secure ratification of the Constitution.

12 To British prime minister William Gladstone, the U.S. Constitution was "the most wonderful work ever struck off at a given time by the brain and purpose of man." But according to Justice Thurgood Marshall, the U.S. Constitution was **"defective** from the start, requiring several amendments, a civil war, and momentous social transformation to attain the system of constitutional

Please note that excerpts and passages in the StudySync® library and this workbook are intended as touchstones to generate interest in an author's work. The excerpts and passages do not substitute for the reading of entire texts, and StudySync® strongly recommends that students seek out and purchase the whole literary or informational work in order to experience it as the author intended. Links to online resellers are available in our digital library. In addition, complete works may be ordered through an authorized reseller by filling out and returning to StudySync® the order form enclosed in this workbook.

Reading & Writing
Companion

55

NOTES

government, and its respect for the individual freedoms and human rights, we hold as fundamental today." The Constitution was not perfect, but rather **perfectible**—through the amendment process.

13 At the Constitutional Convention, Benjamin Franklin stated that he approved of the Constitution "with all its faults" because he did not think a better one was possible at that time. The oldest delegate to the convention at eighty-one, Franklin was too weak to give speeches and instead offered his opinions through written remarks delivered by a fellow Pennsylvania delegate. Franklin reportedly signed the Constitution with tears in his eyes. But if Franklin was willing to sign a document so full of errors, according to one tart-tongued Boston critic, "no wonder he shed a tear." Perhaps Franklin's last words to the convention gave the best assessment of the prospects of the new republic. As the other delegates were signing the Constitution, Franklin remarked to those nearby that, throughout the convention, he had wondered whether the sun carved on the back of George Washington's chair was rising or setting. "Now," he said, "I have the happiness to know that it is a rising and not a setting sun."

Excerpted from *The Words We Live By: Your Annotated Guide to the Constitution* by Linda Monk, published by Hachette Books.

THINK QUESTIONS   CA-CCSS: CA.RI.7.1, CA.L.7.4a, CA.L.7.4b, CA.SL.7.1a, CA.SL.7.1c, CA.SL.7.1d

1. Why are the first three words of the Constitution ("We the People") the most important words in the document? Cite specific evidence from paragraph 2 to support your answer.

2. In paragraph 4, what reasons does Justice Thurgood Marshall give for his view that the first three words of the Preamble are evidence "of the evolving nature of the Constitution"? What specific evidence does the author provide in paragraph 5 to support Marshall's viewpoint? Cite textual evidence to support your answer.

3. Explain why the Antifederalists were worried about ratifying the Constitution. How did the Federalists convince them to support ratification?

Cite evidence from paragraph 11 to support your response.

4. Use context clues to determine the meaning of the word **defective** as it is used in paragraph 12. Write your definition of "defective." Explain how you figured out the meaning of the word by citing specific evidence from the text.

5. Remembering that the Latin suffix *-ible* means "capable of," use the context clues provided in the passage to determine the meaning of **perfectible** in paragraph 12. Write your definition of "perfectible" and explain how you determined the meaning of the word.

CLOSE READ

CA-CCSS: CA.RI.7.1, CA.RI.7.2, CA.RI.7.4, CA.RI.7.5, CA.RI.7.7, CA.L.7.4a, CA.L.7.4c, CA.L.7.5c, CA.W.7.2a, CA.W.7.2b, CA.W.7.2c, CA.W.7.2d, CA.W.7.2e, CA.W.7.2f, CA.W.7.4, CA.W.7.5, CA.W.7.6, CA.W.7.10

Reread the excerpt from *The Words We Live By*. As you reread, complete the Focus Questions below. Then use your answers and annotations from the questions to help you complete the Writing Prompt.

FOCUS QUESTIONS

1. Use the following link to access the StudySync audio version of *The Words We Live By*. Listen to the audio for paragraphs 1–4, including the quotation (0:22–1:32) by Thurgood Marshall. Highlight the word the actor stresses in the first sentence of paragraph 3. Make annotations to explain why the actor might have stressed this word.

2. Highlight the text structure that Monk uses in paragraph 12. Make annotations paraphrasing what she is comparing and contrasting. With which person do you agree—Gladstone or Marshall? Cite specific evidence from the text to support your reasons.

3. Monk makes a strong case for the idea that "We the People" was not an accurate phrase to use in the Preamble to the Constitution because the document excluded many people in American society. Reread paragraphs 1–5. Highlight the groups of people in paragraph 3 who were not included in this document. Then use the following link to access the StudySync audio version of *The Words We Live By*. Listen to the audio for paragraphs 1–5 (0:00–2:05) Make annotations explaining which version—print or audio—helped you better understand what the phrase "We the People" connotes, and why it was inaccurate, given its historical context.

4. In the third sentence of paragraph 7, highlight the words "draftsman" and "architect." Use a dictionary to find the denotation of each word. Ask yourself: How was Morris the draftsman and Madison the architect of the Constitution? Distinguish among the connotations of these two words that have a similar meaning, or denotation. Make annotations recording your reasoning.

5. In the last paragraph, Monk describes the Boston critic as "tart-tongued." What is the connotation of the phrase "tart-tongued"? Which context clues helped you figure out the connotation and whether its meaning is neutral, positive, or negative in this context? Make annotations explaining how you determined the connotation of the phrase.

WRITING PROMPT

Listen to the audio version of *The Words We Live By* in StudySync.com
Compare and contrast the printed text version of the selection with the audio version, which has the same content. Focus your writing on the following questions:

- How are the two versions alike?
- How are they different?
- How does the medium affect the impact of the words?
- How does it shape the message or central idea?
- How does the delivery of the words affect the meaning of the selection and how you understand it?
- How does the medium affect how you experience or enjoy the material?

Begin with a clear thesis statement. Support your writing with specific evidence from both the text and audio versions of *The Words We Live By,* using precise language. Use transitions to show clear connections between the versions. Use a formal style, and end with a strong conclusion to support your information.

I, TOO, SING AMERICA

POETRY
Langston Hughes
1925

INTRODUCTION

Born in Joplin Missouri, (James Mercer) Langston Hughes was an influential figure during the Harlem Renaissance, where he helped pioneer a new literary art form called jazz poetry. Inspired by Carl Sandburg and Walt Whitman, Hughes wrote poems that gave voice to his own experiences and the shared experiences of other African-Americans during the era of segregation. "I, Too, Sing America" starts as a personal statement and extends to inspire future generations.

"They'll see how beautiful
I am..."

 FIRST READ

1 I, too, sing America.

2 I am the **darker** brother.

3 They send me to eat in the kitchen

4 When **company** comes,

5 But I laugh,

6 And eat well,

7 And grow strong.

8 **Tomorrow,**

9 I'll be at the table

10 When company comes.

11 Nobody'll **dare**

12 Say to me,

13 "Eat in the kitchen,"

14 Then.

NOTES

15 Besides,

16 They'll see how beautiful I am

17 And be **ashamed**—

18 I, too, am America.

"I, Too" from THE COLLECTED POEMS OF LANGSTON HUGHES by Langston Hughes, edited by Arnold Rampersad with David Roessel, Associate Editor, copyright © 1994 by the Estate of Langston Hughes. Used by permission of Alfred A. Knopf, an imprint of the Knopf Doubleday Publishing Group, a division of Random House LLC. All rights reserved.

 THINK QUESTIONS CA-CCSS: CA.RL.7.1, CA.L.7.4a, CA.L.7.4d

1. Who is the speaker of the poem? How do you know? Refer to one or more details from the beginning of the text to support your response.

2. What is the speaker comparing in lines 2–4 and 8–10? How are these two sets of lines similar? How are they different? How does the second group of lines act as a response to the first set of lines? Cite specific textual evidence to support your answer.

3. Why will those who made him "eat in the kitchen", in line 3, "be ashamed" in the future? Cite specific evidence from the text to support your response.

4. The word **company** is a multiple-meaning word. Use context clues to determine the meaning of "company" as it is used in line 4 and repeated in line 10 in "I, Too, Sing America." Write your definition of "company" and cite the clues you used in the text to help you figure out the meaning.

5. Based on the context of the poem, what do you think the word **dare** in line 11 means? Write your definition of "dare" and confirm the meaning in a print or online dictionary.

Please note that excerpts and passages in the StudySync® library and this workbook are intended as touchstones to generate interest in an author's work. The excerpts and passages do not substitute for the reading of entire texts, and StudySync® strongly recommends that students seek out and purchase the whole literary or informational work in order to experience it as the author intended. Links to online resellers are available in our digital library. In addition, complete works may be ordered through an authorized reseller by filling out and returning to StudySync® the order form enclosed in this workbook.

Reading & Writing Companion   61

CLOSE READ

CA-CCSS: CA.RL.7.1, CA.RL.7.2, CA.RL.7.4, CA.RL.7.5, CA.RL.7.7, CA.L.7.5a, CA.W.7.2a, CA.W.7.2b, CA.W.7.2c, CA.W.7.2d, CA.W.7.2e, CA.W.7.2f, CA.W.7.4, CA.W.7.5, CA.W.7.6, CA.W.7.10

Reread the poem "I, Too, Sing America." As you reread, complete the Focus Questions below. Then use your answers and annotations from the questions to help you complete the Writing Prompt.

FOCUS QUESTIONS

Questions 2, and 4 ask you to use documents located on the web. Ask your teacher for URLs to find these documents.

1. In "I Hear America Singing," Walt Whitman uses the idea of "America singing" as a metaphor. One interpretation of this metaphor is that it stands for telling one's story of America and of being heard. Another interpretation is that it represents the participation of Americans in their society. Both meanings support Whitman's metaphor that all Americans, regardless of their position in society, have the freedom to "sing," to be heard, and to participate in the building of America. Highlight evidence in "I, Too, Sing America" that supports the idea that Hughes is making an allusion to Whitman's metaphor. Make annotations to support your analysis.

2. Reread the poem. Then listen to Denzel Washington's reading of "I, Too, Sing America" at. Where does the poem have a shift in focus and structure? Highlight this line in the printed text. Make annotations explaining how Denzel Washington's reading of the line alerts the reader to the shift in structure and theme in the poem.

3. Free verse often uses assonance (the repetition of vowel sounds in nearby words) and alliteration (the repetition of consonant sounds at the beginning of nearby words) to produce interesting sounds in a poem. Reread lines 15–17. Highlight the use of assonance and alliteration in some of the words. Make annotations explaining why a poem written in free verse might rely on assonance and alliteration to create a pleasing sound and rhythm in a poem.

4. Listen again to Denzel Washington's reading of "I, Too, Sing America" at. Focus on the last line of the poem (0:42–0:47). Highlight this line in the printed text and make annotations describing how the spoken presentation adds to your understanding of the theme of the poem.

5. Highlight evidence in the text that suggests that Hughes is using the metaphor of a home to explore his theme of the African American hope for racial equality in the future. Do you think that this metaphor works in the poem? How effective is his portrayal of America as an unjust society waiting for change? Make annotations explaining your response.

WRITING PROMPT

What is the central theme of "I, Too, Sing America"? In a clear thesis statement, explain how Langston Hughes uses the open form of free verse, alliteration and assonance, and figurative language, such as allusion and metaphor, to develop the theme of the poem. In what ways does hearing the poem recited affect your understanding of it and the theme? Focus your writing on these questions:

- How are the print and the audio versions alike?
- How are they different?
- How does the medium affect the impact of the words?
- How does it shape the message or theme?
- How does the delivery of the words affect the meaning of the poem and how you understand it?
- How does the medium affect how you experience or enjoy the material?

Begin with a clear thesis statement. Support your writing with specific evidence from both the text and audio versions, using precise language. Use transitions to show clear connections between the versions. Maintain a formal style, and end with a strong conclusion to support your writing.

Please note that excerpts and passages in the StudySync® library and this workbook are intended as touchstones to generate interest in an author's work. The excerpts and passages do not substitute for the reading of entire texts, and StudySync® strongly recommends that students seek out and purchase the whole literary or informational work in order to experience it as the author intended. Links to online resellers are available in our digital library. In addition, complete works may be ordered through an authorized reseller by filling out and returning to StudySync® the order form enclosed in this workbook.

Reading & Writing Companion   **63**

REALITY TV AND SOCIETY

NON-FICTION
2014

INTRODUCTION

In these two articles, the writers make arguments for and against reality TV shows. One writer discusses the negative impacts of shows like *Jersey Shore* and *Here Comes Honey Boo Boo*, while the other focuses on the positive influence of shows like *American Idol* and *Supernanny*. Both writers present strong arguments and support their claims with evidence. Which of the writers' arguments do you find to be more convincing?

"...if what Americans see on reality TV is truly who we are, then we are in big trouble."

 FIRST READ

Reality TV Shows: Harmless Entertainment or Bad Influence?

Point: Stop Rewarding Bad Behavior

1   Television has been an important part of American life for nearly seven decades. But instead of improving with age, programming has **degenerated** into mindless reality TV. Even though these programs claim to picture real people in real situations, there is actually very little *real* in reality TV. There is, however, a real influence on TV viewers, and this influence is often negative, especially on young people. Many people claim that reality TV portrays an accurate and vivid picture of our society. But if what Americans see on reality TV is truly who we are, then we are in big trouble.

2   According to Nielsen, a television ratings company, in 2014 nearly 300 million Americans ages two and up live in homes with televisions. That figure represents more than 90 percent of the population who have access to hundreds of channels and the programs they show. Unfortunately, ratings show that many television viewers are choosing *Here Comes Honey Boo Boo* over political talk shows, broadcasts of national political conventions, or other programming reflecting issues that affect us all.

3   Of course, reality TV has turned many people into instant celebrities. Viewers see that people without talent or hard work can become rich and famous. All they have to do is behave badly in front of the camera. But what message does this send to young people? According to Russ Rankin, who often writes for the arts, young people are not viewing reality TV as mindless entertainment. They look up to the programs' stars and imitate them. They are easily influenced by what they see, and they see that bad behavior is rewarded. Young viewers learn that those who treat others with pettiness and contempt become rich and famous. In fact, in 2011, one of the stars of *Jersey Shore* was

Please note that excerpts and passages in the StudySync® library and this workbook are intended as touchstones to generate interest in an author's work. The excerpts and passages do not substitute for the reading of entire texts, and StudySync® strongly recommends that students seek out and purchase the whole literary or informational work in order to experience it as the author intended. Links to online resellers are available in our digital library. In addition, complete works may be ordered through an authorized reseller by filling out and returning to StudySync® the order form enclosed in this workbook.

Reading & Writing Companion   **65**

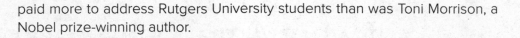

paid more to address Rutgers University students than was Toni Morrison, a Nobel prize-winning author.

4   Tom Green is a comedian and actor who benefited from reality TV. Yet he is one of the most vocal voices against the genre. The difference for him, he says, is that he was not **exploited** and was in charge of his program. As the demand increased for more outrageous and negative programs, Green saw that "the audience became addicted to the cheap thrills." The quality of TV degenerated. He says, "The days of looking up to inventors, artists, and genuinely successful people are gone. Most people assume the behavior they see on TV is acceptable simply because it is on TV in the first place. Our media is shaping culture and training the audience to no longer demand quality programming. I had always presumed that the major corporations that ruled our media were far more responsible than I. Apparently, I was wrong."

5   Television producer Michael Slezak, senior editor of TVLine.com, says that he thinks reality TV shows are so prevalent because "networks love a good reality show since they're less expensive to produce. They don't require drawing in big stars."

6   It seems that no matter how often people are told that what they are watching is far from reality, they still watch. They continue to nurture false expectations that they too could become rich and famous if only they could be selected to participate in reality TV. In a recent survey, 10 percent of British teenagers were motivated by the dream of money and success. They said they would give up a good education to become a reality TV star.

7   It's not really the job of television networks to police the influences of television on culture and society. Yet networks do need to take some responsibility for what they have created with reality TV. As Tom Green says, "The networks should self-regulate by putting power back into the hands of artists and comedians." The media has done a massively good job of influencing society against smoking. They are now working on educating the public about obesity and healthy eating habits. They should be just as concerned about influencing the public about intelligent viewing and showing the best of how people should treat one another.

Counterpoint: Reality TV Can Educate and Inspire

8   Which came first: the chicken or the egg? This age-old question can easily be applied to the **controversy** surrounding reality television. Have these shows **corrupted** our society? Or do they reflect the natural changes that have occurred in the way we see our world?

9   Most people who claim that reality TV has had a negative effect on society are mainly referring to shows that focus on celebrities, such as *Keeping Up With the Kardashians*, or on contrived competitions such as *Survivor*. *Survivor* can be said to build teamwork, but the challenges the contestants face are admittedly not real. And even though the participants are not in any real danger, they are encouraged to create drama to thrill viewers.

10   Other competitive reality TV shows truly showcase talent. Programs such as *Project Runway, American Idol, America's Got Talent,* and *So You Think You Can Dance* give artists and performers the chance to appear before millions of TV viewers. As a result, the careers of many participants have been launched by way of these programs, even though these contestants did not win the competition. One dancer from Texas, for example, has danced professionally in music videos and on TV shows such as *Glee* since appearing on *So You Think You Can Dance.* These shows inspire young viewers. They see people like them succeeding. So they may think, "I can do that." In this way, reality shows encourage young people to reach for the stars.

11   Reality shows that focus on the lives of everyday people may also give people comfort. As the Greek philosopher Aristotle once said of those who attended theater performances, they did so "to be cured, relieved, restored to psychic health." Viewers can identify with people who seem just like them. They see people with problems similar to (or worse than) their own. As a result, they may realize that their own struggles are not as bad as they thought.

12   Reality TV also introduces viewers to lifestyles, cultures, and people different from themselves. The NAACP reported in 2008 that reality programs are the only segment of television that fairly represents nonwhite groups. At least the people viewers see reflect the wide **diversity** of people in our nation.

13   Some reality TV shows actually improve society. For example, shows such as *Hoarders* increase public awareness of a serious mental health problem. Other shows, such as *Supernanny,* give parents and caregivers tips on how to handle children.

14   Blaming reality TV for society's challenges is a convenient way to avoid taking a hard look at ourselves and finding solutions to our problems. Life is messy, and reality TV honestly reveals that truth. Once we realize that we are far from perfect, we can learn to accept others for who they are. Certainly, acceptance of others, with all their faults, is a big step toward creating a better society for everyone.

THINK QUESTIONS   CA-CCSS: CA.RI.7.1, CA.L.7.4a, CA.L.7.4b, CA.L.7.4d

1. What position does the "Point" author take in the debate over reality TV? Cite two pieces of evidence from the "Point" essay to support your answer.

2. The "Point" author uses the opinion of comedian Tom Green to support the argument. How does Green's opinion help the author explain what has caused the quality of TV to decline? Cite specific evidence from the fourth paragraph of the "Point" essay to support your answer.

3. What position does the "Counterpoint" author take in the debate over reality TV? Cite two pieces of evidence from the fifth and sixth paragraph of the "Counterpoint" essay to support your response.

4. Use context clues to determine the meaning of the word **degenerated** as it is used in the first paragraph of the Point section in "Reality TV and Society." Write your definition of "degenerated" and identify the clues that helped you figure out the meaning. Look up the word in a dictionary to confirm or revise your definition.

5. Use context clues in the sentence and in surrounding sentences to determine the meaning of the word **controversy** as it is used in the first paragraph of the Counterpoint section in "Reality TV and Society." Write your definition of "controversy." Then look up the definition in a dictionary to confirm or revise your meaning. Tell how you determined the meaning of the word, explaining how your definition supports the idea of a debate between the two authors in the text.

CLOSE READ
CA-CCSS: CA.RI.7.1, CA.RI.7.6, CA.RI.7.8, CA.RI.7.9, CA.W.7.1a, CA.W.7.1b, CA.W.7.1c, CA.W.7.1d, CA.W.7.1e, CA.W.7.4, CA.W.7.5, CA.W.7.6, CA.W.7.10

Reread the debate "Reality TV and Society." As you reread, complete the Focus Questions below. Then use your answers and annotations from the questions to help you complete the Writing Prompt.

FOCUS QUESTIONS

1. How does the "Point" author use the first paragraph and the "Counterpoint" author the third paragraph of their essays to establish their purpose and point of view? How does each author distinguish his or her position on reality TV from that of the other writer, even though they are writing about the same topic? Highlight relevant evidence from the text. Make annotations to compare and contrast the different points of view that the two authors express about the same topic.

2. In paragraph 4, the "Point". author quotes the comedian Tom Green. In what ways does Green support the "Point" author's argument? Highlight your textual evidence and make annotations to explain your ideas.

3. Trace and evaluate the specific claim in paragraph 5 under "Point: Stop Rewarding Bad Behavior." How does it differ from the other evidence this author has presented up to this point? Do the reasons and evidence support the author's claim? Why or why not? Highlight textual evidence and make annotations to support your answer.

4. Reread paragraph 6 under "Point: Stop Rewarding Bad Behavior" and paragraph 3 under "Counterpoint: Reality TV Can Educate and Inspire." Which author has convinced you of his or her argument? Is reality TV good or bad for society? Evaluate the merit and reasonableness of the claim offered by the author you chose. Highlight evidence from the text and make annotations to support your response.

5. Based on the evidence in paragraph 2 under "Counterpoint: Reality TV Can Educate and Inspire," what do you think the author's point of view is on reality shows such as *Keeping Up With the Kardashians* and *Survivor?* Support your point of view with strong reasons. Highlight relevant evidence from the text and be sure that it's sufficient. Make annotations to highlight the evidence you found most convincing.

WRITING PROMPT

You have read the opposing viewpoints in the article titled "Are Reality Shows Good for Society?" With which author's point of view do you agree? Are reality shows bad or beneficial for society? Use transitions to show relationships between ideas. In your opinion, which author made the stronger argument? Which writer was more convincing? Why? How strong was the author's reasons and evidence? Support your own writing with clear reasons and relevant evidence from the text to explain why one author and not the other persuaded you to accept his or her point of view about the influence of reality TV on society. Maintain a formal writing style and end with a strong conclusion.

A ROLE TO PLAY

English Language Development

FICTION

INTRODUCTION

On a day like any other day in science class, Bryan gets unwelcome news. He is assigned a role for a group project. He doubts his own abilities as he thinks back to a role he was assigned for a group project in sixth grade. He had wanted to do well, but he let his group down. Now Bryan must confront his fears and fulfill his role. Can he do it?

"He could already feel his heart thumping erratically. *Group project? Roles?* he thought. *Anything but that.*"

 FIRST READ

1 Bryan made his way to his lab stool in the third row. It was another day of fifth-period science. "Next week, we will be finishing our unit on the **environment** and **conservation**," Mrs. Jesky said. "Therefore, it's time to show what you've learned. You will be completing a group project on conservation. Each person in the group will be assigned a role. Your role will help the group complete the project."

2 At once, Bryan felt his palms become damp. He told himself to breathe. He could already feel his heart thumping **erratically**. *Group project? Roles?* he thought. *Anything but that.* It was like being back in sixth-grade language arts. Bryan and his group had to prepare a presentation on *Sadako and the Thousand Paper Cranes*. Their teacher, Mr. Mack, gave each person a role. It was Bryan's job to pick important passages from the text and explain their significance. From the start, Bryan was **nervous**. He wasn't sure how to do his task. His group asked about his progress. He said he was almost done. But it was a lie. A year later, he still felt guilty for letting his group down.

3 Back in fifth period, Bryan tried to focus. He looked around tentatively. Mrs. Jesky was still explaining the details of the project. "With your group, you will be creating a web page to explain your idea for a community conservation project," Mrs. Jesky explained. "I will be assigning each of you a role based on your strengths and interests."

4 When Bryan left class that day, he was preoccupied with the science project. Mrs. Jesky gave Bryan the role of **webmaster**. It was his job to take the group's information and ideas and put them into a website. *Why webmaster? Why not researcher? Why not spokesperson?* He wasn't sure he could do the job. It was sixth-grade language arts all over again.

5 Bryan walked unusually slowly into science class the next day. Mrs. Jesky noticed the change in his demeanor. "Bryan, what's wrong?" she asked.

6 "It's the project," he said. "I don't think I can do it."

7 Mrs. Jesky said, "Bryan, I gave you that role for a good reason. You have a talent for presenting information in a way that people understand. For example, the videos and presentations you are making for Ms. Reed's art club are really fine!"

8 For several moments, Bryan thought about what Mrs. Jesky said. He smiled. "Maybe you're right," he said. "I really do like making those videos. And people have told me they are good. Maybe I can be a good webmaster."

9 Mrs. Jesky smiled. "I know you can."

USING LANGUAGE   CA-CCSS: ELD.PII.7.2.b.Ex

Choose the connecting word or phrase in each of the following passages.

1. "Next week, we will be finishing our unit on the environment and conservation," Mrs. Jesky said. "Therefore, it's time to show what you've learned . . ."

    ○ on   ○ Therefore

2. Bryan walked unusually slowly into science class the next day.

    ○ unusually slowly   ○ the next day

3. "You have a talent for presenting information in a way that people understand. For example, the videos and presentations you are making for Ms. Reed's art club are really fine!"

    ○ You have   ○ For example

4. For several moments, Bryan thought about what Mrs. Jesky said. He smiled.

    ○ For several moments   ○ He smiled.

5. "I really do like making those videos. And people have told me they are good."

    ○ I really do   ○ And

MEANINGFUL INTERACTIONS CA-CCSS: ELD.PII.7.1.Ex

Read each excerpt from "A Role to Play." With your partner, circle the words and phrases in each paragraph excerpt that introduce a character into the story. Then underline the words and phrases that tell about the settings. Explain to your partner the reasons for your choices. Then use the self-assessment rubric to evaluate your participation in the assigned task.

1 Bryan made his way to his lab stool in the third row. It was another day of fifth-period science. "Next week, we will be finishing our unit on the environment and conservation," Mrs. Jesky said. "Therefore, it's time to show what you've learned. You will be completing a group project on conservation."

2 *Group project? Roles?* he thought. *Anything but that.* It was like being back in sixth-grade language arts. Bryan and his group had to prepare a presentation on *Sadako and the Thousand Paper Cranes*. Their teacher, Mr. Mack, gave each person a role. It was Bryan's job to pick important passages from the text and explain their significance. From the start, Bryan was nervous. He wasn't sure how to do his task. His group asked about his progress.

3 Back in fifth period, Bryan tried to focus. He looked around tentatively. Mrs. Jesky was still explaining the details of the project.

5 Bryan walked unusually slowly into science class the next day. Mrs. Jesky noticed the change in his demeanor. "Bryan, what's wrong?" she asked.

SELF-ASSESSMENT RUBRIC CA-CCSS: ELD.PII.7.1.Ex

	4 I did this well.	3 I did this pretty well.	2 I did this a little bit.	1 I did not do this.
I took an active part with my partner in doing the assigned task.				
I contributed effectively to the decisions.				
I understood where new characters and settings were introduced in the selection.				
I helped my partner understand where new characters and settings were introduced in the selection.				
I accurately circled and underlined the places in which new characters and settings were introduced.				

REREAD

Reread "A Role to Play." After you reread, complete the Using Language and Meaningful Interactions activities.

USING LANGUAGE   CA-CCSS: ELD.PII.7.3.Ex

For questions 1–3, rewrite each sentence using the correct present progressive tense of the verb in parentheses. For questions 4–6, rewrite each sentence using the correct future progressive tense of the verb in parentheses.

1. Bryan (make) his way to his lab stool in the third row.

   _____

2. Bryan (feel) his palms become damp.

   _____

3. Those videos and presentations you (make) are great.

   _____

4. With your group, you (create) a web page.

   _____

5. Mrs. Jesky (base) project roles on students' strengths and interests.

   _____

6. Mrs. Jesky (explain) the details of the project.

   _____

👥 MEANINGFUL INTERACTIONS   CA-CCSS: ELD.PI.7.3.Ex, ELD.PI.7.11.a.Ex

From what you have read in "A Role to Play," do you think job assignments are important to achieving success on a project? In your small group, practice sharing and discussing your opinions, each of you taking a side of the question and using the speaking frames. Then use the self-assessment rubric to evaluate your participation in the discussion.

- In my opinion, job assignments are . . . because . . .

- Why do you think job assignments are . . . ?

- I think you said that . . .

- I agree / don't agree with that because . . .

🔲 SELF-ASSESSMENT RUBRIC   CA-CCSS: ELD.PI.7.3.Ex, ELD.PI.7.11.a.Ex

	4 I did this well.	3 I did this pretty well.	2 I did this a little bit.	1 I did not do this.
I expressed my opinion clearly.				
I listened carefully to others' opinions.				
I spoke respectfully when disagreeing with others.				
I was courteous when persuading others to share my view.				

REREAD

Reread "A Role to Play." After you reread, complete the Using Language and Meaningful Interactions activities.

 USING LANGUAGE CA-CCSS: ELD.PII.7.5.Ex

Each sentence has two adverbials that tell *how*, *when*, *where*, or *why*. Write the two correct adverbials for each sentence in the second and third columns.

Adverbial 1 Options		Adverbial 2 Options	
soon	really	in art club	to make the right choice
unhappily	next week	finally	badly
now		thoroughly	

Sentence	Adverbial 1	Adverbial 2
By the end of _____, we _____ will be finishing our unit on the environment and conservation.		
Right _____, Mrs. Jesky is explaining the details of the project very _____.		
Bryan is thinking _____ about last year's language arts project and about letting down his group so _____.		
Mrs. Jesky will be assigning roles _____. She will be considering students' strengths and interests _____.		
People _____ like the videos and presentations Bryan is making _____.		

MEANINGFUL INTERACTIONS CA-CCSS: ELD.PI.7.3.Ex

Why do you think assigned jobs are important or not important to the success of a project? Work in small groups to practice sharing and discussing your opinions. Use the speaking frames as a guide. Use information from the story and from your own experience to support your opinion.

- My opinion is that assigned jobs are . . . because . . .

- My opinion is based on . . .

- This evidence indicates that . . .

- Therefore, I think . . .

SCHOOL LUNCHES

WHO DECIDES WHAT STUDENTS SHOULD EAT?

English Language Development

NON-FICTION

INTRODUCTION

I n these two articles, writers make arguments for and against healthful school lunch programs. One writer argues that healthful school lunch programs benefit students. The other argues that taking away unhealthful options also takes away students' power of choice. After reading their arguments, what will you decide? Should schools determine what students eat for lunch, or should students have the final say?

"Many students were reluctant to try the healthful lunches. They wanted to eat salty chips and sweet cookies."

FIRST READ

NOTES

Point: New Programs Provide Healthful, Delicious Options

1 School lunches are changing in the United States. Many groups advocate for more **healthful** lunches. They work hard to change the rules about what kinds of foods are in school cafeterias. They want schools to replace hamburgers, greasy fries, high-fat pizza, and other foods like these. Instead, they want schools to have more healthful options. They suggest whole grains, fruits, and vegetables. They want students to be healthier and stronger.

2 Many students were reluctant to try the healthful lunches. They wanted to eat salty chips and sweet cookies. They did not want carrots and oranges. Then the protests got quieter. Schools say that over time, students happily started eating the healthful foods. Many schools now offer salad bars, which allow students to make healthful salads. They can top crispy lettuce with **tart** tomatoes, **hearty** black beans, or sweet peaches. Now students embrace more healthful options.

3 Healthful school lunches don't benefit students just during lunch. They benefit students all day and beyond. The U.S. Department of Agriculture (USDA) says that students who eat more healthful lunches are more likely to eat less sugar and be more physically active. For the good of our students—our most valuable resource—our schools should have healthful school lunches.

Counterpoint: New Rules Limit Student Choice

4 Groups want to limit the choices students have in school cafeterias across the United States. These groups want to take away foods students like. They want to take away pizza, chips, and soda. They want to replace these foods with salads, whole wheat pasta, and other less popular foods. These groups say that taking away "unhealthful" foods will help improve students' diets.

5   But these new rules leave many students hungry. Many students who eat the more healthful school lunches say the food doesn't taste good. Who wants to eat **bitter, soggy** broccoli when he or she could have chicken nuggets? As a result, students throw a lot of food in the trash. Students also say they are hungry by the end of the day. When students are hungry, they are more tired and more distracted in class.

6   More importantly, the new rules limit students' choices. Students no longer have the right to choose what they eat. Some schools have banned the sale of chips, candy, and soda. These foods aren't even available in school vending machines. Many say that this lack of choice takes away students' rights. Who should have the power to choose which foods are on lunch trays: schools or the students who have to eat those foods?

⚙ USING LANGUAGE CA-CCSS: ELD.PI.7.12.b.Ex

The chart shows sentences from paragraph 5 of "School Lunches: Who Decides What Students Should Eat?" For each row, read the sentence from the text and the directions for writing a new sentence that has a similar meaning. Then fill in the blank to write the new sentence.

Sentence from Text	Directions for New Sentence	New Sentence
But these changes cause problems.	Fill in the blank to complete the sentence with a comparative adjective formed from the word "hard."	Changes in school lunch programs make things _____ for students.
Many students who eat the more healthful school lunches say the food doesn't taste good.	Fill in the blank to complete the sentence with a phrase that means "more healthful."	Many students who eat the lunches that are _____ say that the food in those lunches doesn't taste good.
Who wants to eat bitter, soggy broccoli when he or she could have chicken nuggets?	Fill in the blank to complete the sentence with a comparative adjective formed from the word "popular."	After all, chicken nuggets are _____ _____ than bitter, soggy broccoli!
Students also say they are hungry by the end of the day.	Fill in the blank to complete the sentence with a comparative adjective formed from the word "hungry."	Students also say the new school lunches leave them _____ than the old school lunches did.
When students are hungry, they are more tired and more distracted in class.	Fill in the blank to complete the sentence with a phrase that means the opposite of "more tired and more distracted."	When students have eaten a healthful breakfast, they are _____ _____ in class.

MEANINGFUL INTERACTIONS CA-CCSS: ELD.PI.7.6.b.Ex

Work with your partner or group to make inferences and draw conclusions about information presented in "School Lunches: Who Decides What Students Should Eat?" Use the speaking frames as support for your discussion. Then use the self-assessment rubric to evaluate your participation in the discussion.

- The text has these details: "They want schools to replace hamburgers, greasy fries, high-fat pizza, and other foods like these. Instead, they want schools to have more healthful options. They suggest whole grains, fruits, and vegetables." These details lead me to make the inference that . . .

- The text has these details: "Many students were reluctant to try the healthful lunches. They wanted to eat salty chips and sweet cookies. They did not want carrots and oranges. Then the protests got quieter." These details lead me to make the inference that students began to . . .

- The text has these details: "Many students who eat the more healthful school lunches say the food doesn't taste good. Who wants to eat bitter, soggy broccoli when he or she could have chicken nuggets?" These details lead me to make the inference that students . . .

- The text has these details: "As a result, students throw a lot of food in the trash. Students also say they are hungry by the end of the day. When students are hungry, they are more tired and more distracted in class." These details lead me to make the inference that the new, healthful lunches . . .

- From all this information, I can draw the conclusion that the new school lunch programs . . .

 SELF-ASSESSMENT RUBRIC CA-CCSS: ELD.PI.7.6.b.Ex

	4 I did this well.	3 I did this pretty well.	2 I did this a little bit.	1 I did not do this.
I took an active part with others in doing the assigned task.				
I contributed effectively to the group's decisions.				
I understood how to use information in the text to express inferences and conclusions.				
I helped others understand how to use information in the text to express inferences and conclusions.				
I completed the inference and conclusion sentences carefully and accurately.				

REREAD

Reread "School Lunches: Who Decides What Students Should Eat?" After you reread, complete the Using Language and Meaningful Interactions activities.

USING LANGUAGE CA-CCSS: ELD.PI.7.12.b.Ex, ELD.PII.7.5.Ex

For each item, look at the adjective. Then, using the adjective, apply your knowledge of the suffix -ly to create an adverb to add detail to the sentence. Write the adverb in the blank.

1. **Adjective: reluctant**

   Students _____ tried the new foods.

2. **Adjective: happy**

   Now, students _____ eat the healthful foods.

3. **Adjective: physical**

   Research shows that students who eat more healthful lunches are more likely to eat less sugar and are more _____ active.

4. **Adjective: glad**

   Not all students eat the new, healthful foods _____.

5. **Adjective: wrong**

   Some say that new school lunch rules _____ take away students' choices.

Please note that excerpts and passages in the StudySync® library and this workbook are intended as touchstones to generate interest in an author's work. The excerpts and passages do not substitute for the reading of entire texts, and StudySync® strongly recommends that students seek out and purchase the whole literary or informational work in order to experience it as the author intended. Links to online resellers are available in our digital library. In addition, complete works may be ordered through an authorized reseller by filling out and returning to StudySync® the order form enclosed in this workbook.

Reading & Writing Companion   **83**

MEANINGFUL INTERACTIONS   CA-CCSS: ELD.PI.7.7.Ex

You have read "School Lunches: Who Decides What Students Should Eat?" In this text, readers encounter two arguments—one in favor of schools offering only healthful lunches and the other in favor of students choosing what they want to eat. As the authors try to persuade readers to accept their positions, they use emotional appeals to support their arguments. Emotional appeals are attempts to get an emotional response or reaction from someone. Use the speaking frames below to evaluate whether each author's language choice supports his or her argument. Then use the self-assessment rubric to evaluate your participation in the discussion.

In paragraph 3, the author uses the signal words "For the good of" to begin an emotional appeal.

- The author's emotional appeal is . . .

- The author makes this appeal to show . . .

- I think the author's language choice supports / does not support the argument because . . .

In paragraph 6, the author uses the signal words "More importantly" to begin an emotional appeal.

- The author's emotional appeal is . . .

- The author makes this appeal to show . . .

- I think the author's language choice supports / does not support the argument because . . .

SELF-ASSESSMENT RUBRIC   CA-CCSS: ELD.PI.7.7.Ex

	4 I did this well.	3 I did this pretty well.	2 I did this a little bit.	1 I did not do this.
I expressed my ideas clearly.				
I listened carefully to others' ideas.				
I spoke respectfully when disagreeing with others.				
I was courteous when persuading others to share my view.				

REREAD

Reread "School Lunches: Who Decides What Students Should Eat?" After you reread, complete the Using Language and Meaningful Interactions activities.

USING LANGUAGE CA-CCSS: ELD.PII.7.5.Ex

Complete the chart by using prepositional phrases to add detail to sentences. For each sentence, look at the purpose for modifying to add detail. Then apply your knowledge of how prepositional phrases can act as adverbs to add detail to the sentence in the right column. Choose the correct prepositional phrase from the options box to complete each sentence.

Prepositional Phrase Options	
for the past decade	with salads and whole wheat pasta
for the good of students' health	in school cafeterias

Purpose for Modifying to Add Detail	Sentence	Prepositional Phrase
to tell where	Certain groups want to limit the choices students have _____ _____.	
to tell when	These groups have worked ___ _____ to make school lunches more healthful.	
to tell how	They want to replace pizza, chips, and soda _____.	
to tell why	They want to improve school lunches _____.	

MEANINGFUL INTERACTIONS CA-CCSS: ELD.PI.7.7.Ex

The article "School Lunches: Who Decides What Students Should Eat?" presents two opposing arguments about school lunches. One way the authors attempt to persuade readers is through the use of emotional appeals. Consider an emotional appeal made by one of the authors. As you work to evaluate whether the author's language choice in the emotional appeal helps support the argument, act out the emotional appeal with a partner. Use the writing frames for support as you plan how you will act out the emotional appeal.

- An emotional appeal used by an author in the text is _____
  _____.

- With this emotional appeal, the author is saying _____
  _____.

- We can show this emotional appeal by _____
  and _____.

- Acting out the author's emotional appeal in this way will help show that the language choices
  do / do not support the argument because _____
  _____.

2:40 PM

🔒 app.studysync.com

ASSIGNMENTS   REVIEW   BINDER   BLASTS   LIBRARY

74%

EXTENDED WRITING PROJECT

dysync

WRITE

ED WRITING PROJECT
NARRATIVE WRITING

Extended Writing Project:
Narrative Writing
by StudySync

1   WRITE

Extended Writing Project Prompt and Directions:

Imagine how you would feel if the government banned
probably find it terribly unfair if the authorities took you
have been reading fiction and nonfiction narratives—im
characters or real people who do not live in fair, or just, Rom
something in common: like the gladiators of ancient Rom
the characters or people in these texts are the victims of un
Think about the principles of an open and just society, and co
closed and unjust society. Then write a fictional narrative (or story)
is seeking justice in an unjust society. Model your story on one of the texts yo
this unit.

Your narrative should include:
- a beginning in which you set the scene
- a clear description of the characters
- a series of clearly described events
- an underlying theme (or message)
- a narrator with a specific point of view

Font   Size   B I Ix A U

NARRATIVE WRITING

WRITING PROMPT

Imagine how you would feel if the government banned your favorite TV show. You would probably find it terribly unfair if the authorities took your show off the air. In this unit, you have been reading fiction and nonfiction narratives—imagined and true stories—about characters or real people who do not live in fair, or just, societies. All these selections have something in common: like the gladiators of ancient Rome or the people of North Korea, the characters or people in these texts are the victims of unfair laws and unjust rulers. Think about the principles of an open and just society, and contrast them with the rules of a closed and unjust society. Then write a fictional narrative (or story) about a character who is seeking justice in an unjust society. Model your story on one of the texts you have read in this unit.

Your narrative should include:

- a beginning in which you set the scene
- a clear description of the characters
- a series of clearly described events
- an underlying theme (or message)
- a narrator with a specific point of view

A **narrative** is the retelling of real or imagined experiences or events. Narratives can be fiction or nonfiction. Fictional narratives are made-up stories and can take the form of novels, short stories, poems, or plays. Nonfiction narratives are true stories, often expressed in memoirs or diary entries, personal essays or letters, autobiographies or biographies, eyewitness accounts or histories. Many narratives have a narrator who tells the story as it unfolds. In nonfiction narratives, the author usually tells the story. In fictional narratives, the narrator may or may not be a character in the story. Good narrative writing uses storytelling techniques, descriptive details, and often a clear sequence of events that are told in the order in which the events happen.

The features of narrative writing include:

- setting
- characters
- plot
- theme
- point of view

As you actively participate in this Extended Writing Project, you will receive more instructions and practice to help you craft each of the elements of narrative writing.

 ## STUDENT MODEL

Before you begin to write your own fictional narrative (or story), begin by reading this story that one student wrote in response to the writing prompt. As you read this student model, highlight and annotate the features of narrative writing that the student included in her fictional narrative.

Theo's Song

Clang, clang, clang! Fifty apprentices toiled away in the infernally hot smithy. Their hammers rang out as they pounded red disks of metal into the things the Community needed—horseshoes, armor, and nails. Fifty young people, their faces taut with concentration, swung their hammers relentlessly. No one spoke because no one could hear a puny human voice over the clamor of the workshop.

Theo was a newly apprenticed blacksmith. The Authorities had only recently assigned him to the smithy. As with all the children in the Community, the day Theo had turned thirteen, the Authorities removed him from the nursery pod where he had spent his first twelve years cared for by the Nanny. The Nanny said nothing as he was taken away.

The Authorities had taken Theo to the Interview Room, where he met an older woman, known as the Decider. She considered Theo carefully. She asked him about his goals and dreams. He gladly talked about his desire to become a songwriter and how his greatest wish was to share his music with the Community.

After the interview, the woman gently squeezed Theo's delicate hand and wished him luck. Following a medical examination, the Authorities pronounced his Assignment. Theo, the slight, sensitive, and musical boy, was to become a blacksmith. He would spend the rest of his life laboring in a hot, noise-filled room where he would likely grow deaf to the music inside him.

That had been the Authorities' intention, as Neema, a fellow apprentice, told Theo later. She was two months older than he and still adjusting to her Assignment. She was surprisingly chatty after a day of swinging a hammer, and even yet had the energy to speak with the others during a meal in the crowded Community Room.

"It's their plan," she explained to Theo in a low voice because she knew that Others were listening. "The Authorities, the Decider—they choose the one task that suits you least. I wanted to be a dancer. Now I'm a blacksmith. You know who gets to dance? The people with two left feet!"

"And people who sing can't even carry a tune," Theo lamented. "I don't get it at all. Why make people so miserable? Why not let us do what we're good at?"

Neema whispered now. "Because they can control us if we're unhappy! The hammers bang all day long. All I can think about is getting a minute of quiet. And some sleep," Neema said, yawning.

That night, Theo thought about Neema's words. He, too, spent the hours of his working day trying to block out the deafening noise around him. He realized that he hadn't heard any music in his head since the day he left the Pod. As a result, even in the quiet Sleep Room, because his ears were ringing so loudly, he could not remember even one tune. It was so unfair, so unjust, so *cruel*, he thought. His chest tightened as he considered never singing again. Just before falling into a dreamless sleep, Theo made a resolution that would change his life.

The next day, Theo approached his station at the smithy with a new purpose. As he wound his fingers around the handle of his hammer, instead of closing himself off to the noise around him, he opened his ears. He paid attention to the sounds of the hammers around him. He noticed patterns of rhythms. He heard how the hammers rang out as they struck. Soon, a song began forming in the back of his mind. He coaxed it forward by changing the rhythm of his own hammering. Now he hammered as if striking a drum instead of a horseshoe. He looked around him.

Copyright © BookheadEd Learning, LLC

The other blacksmiths had their heads down over their work. But now words were forming in Theo's mind. A moment later, he threw back his head and sang out:

"Oh, a hammer is a powerful tool! A hammer can shape the world! Yes, a hammer can change the world! You know it, too!"

His voice cracked, but he didn't care. He wanted only to release the song. He pounded his hammer in time with the words and shouted out the notes. Some blacksmiths around him joined in singing, transforming their hammering into a powerful percussion section. Soon, the room echoed with singing so loud that it nearly drowned out the hammering. When the song ended, Theo heard laughter. Someone shouted, "Great song!"

Within minutes, the Authorities collected Theo and led him back to the Interview Room where the older woman sat waiting at a table.

"What you have done is not acceptable, Theo," she told him. "The Authorities decide who may sing and who may not. Your role is to make things."

But Theo was not afraid. He said simply, "Singing makes people happy."

The woman said, "I am sorry for what must happen next, Theo." One of the Authorities entered the room and placed a black thread loosely around Theo's neck. "This thread has the power to cancel human speech. You will not be able to speak—or sing—for one month," the woman said before she dismissed him.

Theo returned to the smithy, where he silently took up his hammer. Word quickly spread of his punishment. Neema was outraged, and decided to take a stand. Within minutes, she was banging her hammer in time and singing Theo's song, and the entire smithy sang along with her. The Authorities were amazed. Never before had they faced such rebellion. They placed a silence thread on Neema and then on others, but song kept breaking out in the smithy. Eventually, the Authorities gave up on the terrible thread. They reassigned some blacksmiths to other tasks, including Theo, who was made a singer. In the end, they did something no one in the Community had ever dreamed of: They assigned all the blacksmithing tasks to apprentices who wanted to take them. Soon the rebellion stopped.

THINK QUESTIONS

1. Where and when might this story take place? What inferences can you make from specific details in the text about the setting and the way in which it affects the plot?

2. What is Theo like? Use specific details in paragraph 3 to describe him. What can you infer about his personality from his physical attributes?

3. Consider what happens to Theo and use time-order (or sequence) words to summarize the key events in the Student Model. How do these events reflect a theme, or central idea, in the story?

4. Think about the writing prompt. Which selections or other resources that you have read or used in this unit would you like to apply to writing your own narrative? What are some ideas that you might like to develop into a story? Make a list of ideas and discuss them with a partner. Support ideas with specific evidence from the texts you have read.

5. Based on what you have read, listened to, or researched, how would you answer the question, "What is it like to live in an unjust society?" Write a paragraph that focuses on a fiction or nonfiction narrative that you could write. Establish a context for action and introduce characters. Address some of the ways that people or characters develop their points of view toward injustice in the world.

PREWRITE

CA-CCSS: CA.W.7.3a, CA.W.7.5, CA.SL.7.1a, CA.SL.7.1b, CA.SL.7.1c, CA.SL.7.1d

WRITING PROMPT

Imagine how you would feel if the government banned your favorite TV show. You would probably find it terribly unfair if the authorities took your show off the air. In this unit, you have been reading fiction and nonfiction narratives—imagined and true stories—about characters or real people who do not live in fair, or just, societies. All these selections have something in common: like the gladiators of ancient Rome or the people of North Korea, the characters or people in these texts are the victims of unfair laws and unjust rulers. Think about the principles of an open and just society, and contrast them with the rules of a closed and unjust society. Then write a fictional narrative (or story) about a character who is seeking justice in an unjust society. Model your story on one of the texts you have read in this unit.

Your narrative should include:

- a beginning in which you set the scene
- a clear description of the characters
- a series of clearly described events
- an underlying theme (or message)
- a narrator with a specific point of view

In addition to studying the techniques authors use to tell stories, you have been reading real and imagined stories about people or characters living in unjust societies. In the extended writing project, you will use those storytelling techniques to compose your own made-up narrative, or story.

Because your story will be about life in an unjust society, you will want to think about how the characters or people you have read about have responded when they have witnessed or participated in an injustice. Think back to when you read "The Lottery": How do the people in the community feel about the lottery? Do they think it is fair or unfair? How do they change as a result of their experiences? What does the narrator think about the lottery and the characters who participate in it? What do you think about a society that has created such a practice? What would you do if you lived in the village?

Make a list of the answers to these questions about "The Lottery." Then consider how at least two other characters you have read about in this unit—for example, Prim's sister in *The Hunger Games* and Jonas in *The Giver*—feel about participating in their societies. As you write down your ideas, look for similarities and differences in the narratives. Do the characters' experiences have anything in common? Do you notice events that are repeated? What do you notice about the narrators who tell these stories? Look for patterns that will help you develop the characters, plot events, including the conflict (or problem) in your story. When you think about how the narrator views the characters and events, you will begin to develop your own point of view. Use this model to help you get started with your own prewriting:

Text: "The Lottery," by Shirley Jackson

How the Characters Feel: *Before the lottery, people in the village are friendly and joking. After the lottery, people become hostile because Tessie Hutchinson says the lottery is unfair. All the other villagers disagree. One says, "All of us took the same chance."*

How the Narrator Feels: *The narrator doesn't seem upset by the events in the story. He or she is just telling the story as a detached or indifferent observer, which is kind of harsh.*

How I Feel: *I think the lottery is scary and unfair. But the people probably have lived in the village for so long that it's an important tradition for them. The lottery must have had a real purpose long ago. However, it seems really unnecessary and cruel now. Like the character Tessie, I would speak up if someone in my family got the paper with the black dot. I would try to save my family member from a terrible, painful end. If I couldn't, I would figure out a way to leave the village.*

After you have completed your prewriting, consider your thoughts and ideas as you work through the following Skills lessons to help you map out your analysis.

SKILL: ORGANIZE NARRATIVE WRITING

⭐ DEFINE

The purpose of writing a narrative is to entertain readers while also inviting them to think about an important theme (or message)—a larger lesson about life or human nature. To convey the theme of a story, writers need to consider how to structure the story and organize the events in a way that makes sense.

Experienced writers carefully choose a **narrative text structure** that best suits their story. Most narratives use chronological (or sequential) text structure. To put it in simpler terms, this organization of a text is also called time order. It means that an author (or narrator) tells the events in the order in which they happen in a story. By telling what happens first, second, third, and so on, an author is giving the sequence of events. Along the way, this text structure enables the author to establish the setting, the characters, and the conflict (or problem) of the plot. Telling the events in time order also allows the characters and the action of the plot to move forward, through the middle of the story, when the main character (or characters) will attempt to resolve the conflict, or solve the problem. Finally, the story ends with the resolution of the conflict.

Sometimes, instead of moving the plot forward in time and action, the plot moves the action backward in time, or even starts the action in the middle of the story. For example, if the story is character-driven, the plot might focus on the character's internal thoughts and feelings, so the writer might begin with a flashback to establish the character's issues or situation before moving into the present time. Similarly, if the story is a mystery, the writer might start the story in the middle to build suspense by making readers question why the person was murdered, for example, and "who done it." To organize their story, writers often use a sequence-of-events chart, a timeline, or a flow chart. This type of graphic organizer will help them visualize and plot the order of events.

NOTES

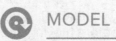IDENTIFICATION AND APPLICATION

- When selecting a text structure for a story, writers consider the theme and the kind of story they want to tell. They consider questions about character and plot events:
  › Should I tell the story in the order that the events happen?
  › Should I use a flashback at the beginning to create mystery and suspense?
  › Who are my characters and how will they grow or change?
  › What is the conflict (or problem) of the plot?
  › What will be the most exciting moment of my story?
  › How will my story end?

- Writers often use signal words to hint at the organizational text structure:
  › Time order: *first, next, then, finally, before, after, now, soon, at last*
  › Cause-effect: *because,* so, *therefore, as a result*
  › Compare-contrast: *like, also* to compare; *unlike, but* to contrast Order of importance: *mainly, most important, to begin with, first*

- Even though a story is usually told in time order, writers may organize individual paragraphs by using a second narrative text structure. For example, when a plot event leads to serious consequences for a character, the writer may use cause-and-effect text structure in a paragraph. Despite these paragraph shifts in text structure, the overall text structure for the story is still time order.

- The sequence of events in a narrative helps shape how a reader responds to what happens, and it also contributes to the overall development of the story's plot from beginning to end. You will learn more about narrative sequencing, and the elements and techniques that move the plot forward, in a later lesson.

MODEL

The writer of the Student Model understood from her prewriting that she would be telling her story in chronological order by giving events in time order—from beginning to end. In this excerpt from the first paragraph of the model, the writer makes the organizational structure clear. The narrator is telling the events in the workshop in the order they happened. However, by using the past tense (e.g., *toiled, rang, swung, spoke*) in the description, the narrator is telling the events to the reader sometime after they happened.

Clang, clang, clang! Fifty apprentices toiled away in the infernally hot smithy. Their hammers rang out as they pounded red disks of metal into the things needed by the Community—horseshoes, armor, and nails. Fifty young people, their faces taut with concentration, swung their hammers relentlessly. No one spoke because no one could hear a puny human voice over the clamor of the workshop.

In the second paragraph, the writer provides some background about the main character, Theo. Therefore, the narrator uses flashback to go back in time to just before the beginning of the story. Notice how the writer changes from using the past tense to the past perfect verb tense ("the day Theo *had turned* thirteen, the Authorities removed him from the nursery pod") to indicate that an event happened in the past ("the day Theo *had turned* thirteen") before another event happened ("the Authorities removed him from the nursery pod"), as well as signal words and phrases—*newly*, and *his first twelve years*—to let readers in on the time shift:

> *Theo was a newly apprenticed blacksmith. The Authorities had only recently assigned him to the smithy. As with all the children in the Community, the day Theo had turned thirteen, the Authorities removed him from the nursery pod where he had spent his first twelve years cared for by the Nanny. The Nanny said nothing as he was taken away.*

After "flashing back" in paragraphs 2 and 3, to fill in Theo's personal history, the writer returns in paragraph 4 to the smithy, the setting of the story, and to where he left off in paragraph 1. The writer uses time-order words and phrases in paragraph 4—*later, still, after, even, yet*— to help readers keep up.

> *That had been the Authorities' intention, as Neema, a fellow apprentice, told Theo later. She was two months older than he and was still adjusting to her Assignment. She was surprisingly chatty after a day of swinging a hammer and even yet had the energy to speak with others during a meal in the crowded Community Room.*

In order to organize the order in which she would tell her events, the writer used an Organize Narrative Writing Timeline. She listed the events and then numbered them in the order in which she first thought that she wanted them to appear in her story.

Event #2: The blacksmiths are working in the smithy.
Event #1: Theo gets taken from the Pod and given his Assignment.
Event #3: Neema explains what the Authorities are doing.
Event #4: Theo makes a resolution.
Event #5: Theo defies the Authorities by singing in the smithy.
Event #6: Theo gets taken to the Decider and punished.
Event #8: The authorities realize they can't control the rebellion and change their ways.
Event #7: Neema and the other blacksmiths continue to rebel by singing.

 PRACTICE

By using an Organize Narrative Writing timeline, you'll be able to fill in the events for your story that you considered in the prewriting stage of your Extended Writing Project. When you are finished, exchange organizers with a partner to offer and receive feedback on the structure of events the writer has planned, and the use of transitions to make shifts in time order and setting clear for the reader.

SKILL:
DESCRIPTIVE
DETAILS

 DEFINE

One way a writer develops the setting, characters, and plot in a narrative is by using description and descriptive details. In a story, the descriptive details help readers imagine the world in which the story takes place and the characters who live in it.

Descriptive details often use precise language—specific nouns and action verbs—to convey experiences or events. Many descriptive details use sensory language to appeal to one or more of the reader's five senses. Sensory words tell how something looks, sounds, feels, smells, or tastes.

Descriptive details should be relevant to the story, such as a character's actions or the setting. In a story, it is easy to include many interesting details, but not every detail is relevant. For example, what a character smells might be less relevant than how he or she feels or what he or she sees or hears during a key moment in the story. Too many details can make the reader feel overwhelmed. Plus, they can slow the pace of a story. It's a good idea to select only the most important, or relevant, details for your story. Think about what the reader really needs to know to understand or picture what is happening. Consider what your narrator actually knows and can share with the reader, especially if he or she is a character in the story. Then choose the details that will most help the readers imagine what the setting looks like, what the characters are experiencing, or how the events are happening.

 IDENTIFICATION AND APPLICATION

One way to generate descriptive details is to use a graphic organizer. It can help you ask questions about your setting, characters, and plot events to determine which details the reader might need to know. The following details in this Descriptive Details Graphic Organizer are from the Student Model, "Theo's Song":

DESCRIPTIVE DETAILS	CHARACTER: THEO	SETTING: SMITHY
Looks like	Young, slender	Full of hard-working apprentices
Sounds like	Voice cracked by thirst	Noisy, full of clanging hammers
Thinks or feels like	Rebellious against the no-singing rules	——
Smells (or tastes) like	——	Like burning metal and hot, sweaty apprentices

As the writer planned the Student Model, she asked some questions to determine which descriptive details would be the most relevant to developing the narrative:

- Will this detail help the reader understand who the character is and why he or she thinks, says, feels, or acts a certain way?
- What does this detail reveal about the narrator's point of view? How does the narrator know this detail? What does the narrator reveal about himself or herself by sharing it?
- Will this detail help the reader experience what the character is feeling?
- Does this detail use language that is interesting and will appeal to one or more of the reader's five senses?
- Will this detail add to the story and help it move forward, or will it slow down the pace of the story?

MODEL

In the following excerpt from the Student Model, the writer uses sensory language to provide relevant descriptive details about the setting. Notice how many of the details appeal to the senses. Think about how vivid, precise language and specific details add to your understanding of the story.

NOTES

Clang, clang, clang! Fifty apprentices toiled away in the infernally hot smithy. Their hammers rang out as they pounded red disks of metal into the things the Community needed—horseshoes, armor, and nails. Fifty young people, their faces taut with concentration, swung their hammers relentlessly. No one spoke because no one could hear a puny human voice over the clamor of the workshop.

The first sentence appeals to the reader's sense of hearing: "Clang, clang, clang!" is an example of onomatopoeia in that the word *clang* actually mimics the sound that the hammers are making as they hit the metal. From the first sentence, readers can tell immediately that the setting is loud and noisy. The second sentence appeals to the sense of touch, smell, or taste: The smithy is hot, and you can almost feel, smell, and taste the heat and sweat. The third sentence includes details that appeal to the sense of hearing ("hammers rang out") and sight ("they pounded red disks of metal"). The fourth sentence appeals to the sense of sight. Because the characters' faces are described as "taut" and their hammers as swinging "relentlessly," you can actually picture the action. The paragraph ends with a sensory detail that appeals to your sense of hearing and helps you imagine how loud the workshop is.

 ## PRACTICE

Create some descriptive details for your story that appeal to the senses. Then trade your details with a partner when you are finished. Offer feedback about the details. Engage in a peer review to determine which details will help keep your story moving forward. Offer feedback on how well sensory details establish context and reveal character point of view.

NOTES

PLAN

CA-CCSS: CA.RL.7.1, CA.RL.7.3, CA.RL.7.6, CA.W.7.3a, CA.W.7.3b, CA.W.7.3d, CA.W.7.4, CA.W.7.5, CA.SL.7.1a, CA.SL.7.1b, CA.SL.7.1c, CA.SL.7.1d

WRITING PROMPT

Imagine how you would feel if the government banned your favorite TV show. You would probably find it terribly unfair if the authorities took your show off the air. In this unit, you have been reading fiction and nonfiction narratives—imagined and true stories—about characters or real people who do not live in fair, or just, societies. All these selections have something in common: like the gladiators of ancient Rome or the people of North Korea, the characters or people in these texts are the victims of unfair laws and unjust rulers. Think about the principles of an open and just society, and contrast them with the rules of a closed and unjust society. Then write a fictional narrative (or story) about a character who is seeking justice in an unjust society. Model your story on one of the texts you have read in this unit.

Your narrative should include:

- a beginning in which you set the scene
- a clear description of the characters
- a series of clearly described events
- an underlying theme (or message)
- a narrator with a specific point of view

Review the ideas you brainstormed in the prewrite activity and then take another look at the events you listed in your Organize Narrative Writing Timeline. Think about what you have learned about audience and purpose and about developing descriptive details for a narrative. These ideas will help you create a road map to use for writing your story.

Consider the following questions as you develop the events of your narrative in the road map and consider the audience and purpose for which you are writing:

- Who are your characters? What are they like?
- Where and when does your story take place?
- Who is telling your story? Is the narrator a character in the story? Or is he or she telling the story from outside the text? What is his or her point of view about the setting, the characters, and the plot?
- What kind of society do your characters live in?
- What problem, or injustice, do they encounter?
- How do your characters resolve the conflict (or problem) of injustice that they face?
- How do your characters grow or change as the story moves forward?
- What is the most exciting moment in your story?
- What happens to your characters at the end?
- What theme (or message) do you want your audience to take away from your story?

Use this graphic organizer to get started with your road map. It has been completed with details from the Student Model, "Theo's Song."

STORY ROAD MAP	
Narrator & Character(s):	Narrator: Someone outside the story Characters: Theo, Neema, the Decider, the Authorities
Setting:	Blacksmith workshop and Community Room of an unknown society
Beginning:	Theo is a thirteen-year-old-boy who wants to become a singer. He is Assigned to be a blacksmith. Theo finds the smithy to be noisy and hot.
Middle:	Neema tells Theo that the Authorities control the people by giving them jobs they are not suited for. Upset at the thought he may never sing again, Theo makes a resolution. At work the next day, he leads the other blacksmiths in song before being taken away by the Authorities. He is punished with a terrible thread that cancels his voice. Neema rebels and leads the blacksmiths when Theo cannot.
End:	The Authorities can't control the rebellion. They re-assign Theo to be among the singers. They give the blacksmith jobs to those people who want them. The society changes to become more fair, or just,

SKILL: INTRODUCTION/ STORY BEGINNING

 DEFINE

The beginning of a fictional narrative is the opening passage in which the writer provides the exposition, or the important details about the story's setting, narrator, characters, plot, conflict, and even the theme. A strong introduction captures the readers' attention by making them want to read on to find out what happens next.

 IDENTIFICATION AND APPLICATION

- The beginning of a narrative (or story) includes exposition. The exposition establishes the setting, the narrator's point of view, the characters, the plot, and even the theme. As in other forms of writing, writers build interest by using a "hook" to capture the reader's interest. In a narrative, a hook can be an exciting moment, a detailed description, or a surprising or thoughtful comment made by the narrator or the main character.

- The beginning of a narrative also establishes the structure of the story. Remember: A story does not have to open with the start of the action. It can begin in the middle. This strategy "grabs" the reader's attention and builds suspense by making the reader wonder what's going on. Some stories even begin at the end and work their way backward in time. These strategies use flashbacks to capture the reader's attention, but they are not necessary. Most good stories start at the beginning of the action and tell the events in time order. They use descriptive supporting details, engaging characters, and unexpected plot twists to keep readers interested.

- The beginning of a story might also offer clues about the theme. The theme is the message or "big idea" about life that the writer wants readers to understand. The theme is developed over the course of the text as the characters grow, change, and make decisions about life. Good writers drop hints at the beginning of the story so that readers can consider the "big idea" as they read.

 MODEL

Reread the first paragraph of Shirley Jackson's famous short story, "The Lottery":

> The morning of June 27th was clear and sunny, with the fresh warmth of a full-summer day; the flowers were blossoming profusely and the grass was richly green. The people of the village began to gather in the square, between the post office and the bank, around ten o'clock; in some towns there were so many people that the lottery took two days and had to be started on June 26th, but in this village, where there were only about three hundred people, the whole lottery took less than two hours, so it could begin at ten o'clock in the morning and still be through in time to allow the villagers to get home for noon dinner.

The author begins by establishing the setting—the time and place in which the plot of the story will unfold. The details about the weather and the village suggest a beautiful summer day in an ordinary small town, with no specific characters being introduced. These details might not "hook" the reader, but then again, what is this lottery? The lottery is mentioned twice in the opening paragraph without any explanation, as if the narrator is "hooking" the readers in the hope of "reeling them in."

As it turns out, the running of the lottery provides the action of the plot, and the outcome of the lottery provides the story's theme—that blindly following tradition is dangerous, especially when it leads to injustice.

Notice that the author has done several key things in the opening paragraph—introduced the setting, or time and place of the story, and given readers an inkling of the conflict of the plot as well as the theme.

PRACTICE

Write a beginning for your story. It should introduce your setting and main character (or characters) and the conflict (or problem) of the plot. Try to include hints that might lead to the theme, or "big idea" about life or human experience. A hint to the theme might be a simple observation that the narrator or the main character makes—or an offhand remark that will turn out to be rich in meaning.

SKILL:
NARRATIVE
TECHNIQUES AND
SEQUENCING

NOTES

 DEFINE

When writing a story, authors use a variety of narrative techniques to develop both the plot and the characters, explore the setting, and engage the reader. These techniques include dialogue, a sequencing of events, pacing, and description. **Dialogue,** what the characters say to one another, is often used to develop characters and move the events of the plot forward. Every narrative contains a **sequence of events,** which is carefully planned and controlled by the author as the story unfolds. Writers often manipulate the **pacing** of a narrative, or the speed with which events occur, to slow down or speed up the action at certain points in a story. This can create tension and suspense. Writers use **description** to build story details and reveal information about the characters, setting, and plot.

The beginning of a story is called the **introduction** or **exposition.** This is the part of the story in which the writer provides the reader with essential information, introducing the characters, the time and place in which the action occurs, and the problem or conflict the characters must face and attempt to solve.

As the story continues, the writer includes details and events to develop the conflict and move the story forward. These events—known as the **rising action** of the story—build until the story reaches its **climax.** This is a turning point in the story, where the most exciting and intense action usually occurs. It is also the point at which the characters begin to find a solution to the problem or conflict in the plot.

The writer then focuses on details and events that make up the **falling action** of the story. This is everything that happens after the climax, leading to a **resolution.** These elements make up a story's **conclusion,** which often contains a message or final thought for the reader.

⬤⬤⬤ IDENTIFICATION AND APPLICATION

- Most narratives are written in sequential order. However, arranging events in time order is not the only skill involved in narrative sequencing. Writers group events to shape both a reader's response to what happens and the development of the plot from beginning to end.
    - *Exposition* refers to the essential information at the start of a story.
    - *Rising action* refers to the sequence of events leading up to a story's turning point.
        - The turning point is called the climax, and it's usually the most suspenseful moment in the story.
        - During the rising action, readers may experience anticipation, curiosity, concern, or excitement.
    - *Falling action* refers to the sequence of events following the story's turning point, or climax, and leading to the resolution of the story's conflict or problem.
        - During the falling action, readers may look forward to finding out how the story will end.
- Pacing is a technique that writers use to control the speed with which events are revealed. Description and dialogue can help writers vary the pacing in a narrative.
- Description uses specific details, precise language, and sensory words to develop characters, setting, and events. It can be used to slow down pacing.
- Dialogue, or the exchange of words between two or more characters, can reveal character traits and important plot details. Dialogue can be used to speed up or slow down pacing. A short, snappy line of dialogue might speed up a story. A long speech might slow it down.
    - Dialogue is set in its own paragraph and inside quotation marks. A line of dialogue might look like this: "My name is Jeannette."
    - Dialogue is usually followed by a tag, such as *she said* or *he asked,* to indicate who is speaking.
    - Dialogue should suit the character who speaks it. Business executives at an important meeting would speak differently from teenagers playing a game at a friend's house.

⟳ MODEL

After the writer gives exposition in the introduction, he or she develops the characters and the events of the story, including the conflict (or problem) that the main character faces. The writer uses description and dialogue to enrich the story and to vary the pacing of events. Some paragraphs are longer than

Copyright © BookheadEd Learning, LLC

NOTES

others. Some include dialogue, and some don't. Some include more descriptive details than others or different types of sentences. By varying the pacing, writers hold readers' interest.

Reread paragraphs 4–7 of the story, which appear in the middle of the Student Model "Theo's Song." Look closely at the text structure and at how the events begin to build the rising action of the story. Notice the writer's use of dialogue, pacing and description and the transitions that help to move the action of the story forward.

That had been the Authorities' intention, as Neema, a fellow apprentice, told Theo **later**. She was two months older than he, and **still** adjusting to her Assignment. She was surprisingly chatty **after** a day of swinging a hammer, and even yet had the energy to engage with others during a meal in the crowded Community Room.

"It's their plan," she explained to Theo in a low voice **because** she knew that Others were listening. "The Authorities, the Decider—they choose the one task that suits you least. I wanted to be a dancer. **Now** I'm a blacksmith. You know who gets to dance? The people with two left feet!"

"And people who sing can't carry a tune," Theo lamented. "I don't get it at all. Why make people so miserable? Why not let us do what we're good at?"

Neema whispered now. "Because they can control us if we're unhappy! The hammers bang all day long. All I can think about is getting a minute of quiet. And some sleep," Neema said, yawning.

That night, Theo thought about Neema's words. He, **too,** spent the hours of his working day trying to block out the deafening noise around him. He realized that he hadn't heard any music in his head **since** the day he left the Pod. As a result, even in the quiet Sleep Room, **because** his ears were ringing so loudly, he could not remember even one tune. It was so unfair, so unjust, so *cruel,* he thought. His chest tightened **as** he considered never singing again. Just **before** falling into a dreamless sleep, Theo made a resolution that would change his life.

Notice how the fourth paragraph of the story (the first body paragraph) focuses on one part of an event—Neema and Theo talking in the Community Room. It includes descriptive details that tell which characters are involved, where they are, and what they are doing or saying. It also includes transition words—*later, still, after*—that indicate time order and that move the action along.

The fifth paragraph of the story features dialogue. All the words are spoken by Neema. A tag "she explained to Theo. . ." tells readers who is speaking and to whom. Notice that when a character speaks, his or her words appear in a new paragraph. As you follow the rest of the conversation, notice how the dialogue sets the stage for events that will likely occur. The writer's use of dialogue also reveals certain qualities about each character. The description of Theo's day, revisited by him as he falls asleep, gives the reader a very distinct impression, both of the setting in which he has found himself, and in the clarity of his feelings toward his situation. Notice the final sentence in the last paragraph. In it, the writer has picked up the pacing of the story. We know that Theo has made a sudden resolution and that it will have a significant impact on his life. The writer unveils this in single sentence intended to move the reader forward into the action with a feeling of suspense and anticipation.

 PRACTICE

Write a paragraph that conveys a point of rising action in your narrative. Focus on one event or one character's dialogue to move your story forward. Use the narrative techniques presented in the lesson, such as description, dialogue, and pacing, to guide readers through your paragraph. Be sure to include descriptive details that will make your story vivid and interesting to your readers.

SKILL:
CONCLUSION/
STORY ENDING

DEFINE

The **conclusion** is the final section of a narrative (or story). It is where the readers find out what happens to the characters. The plot winds down, and the main character's conflict (or problem) is resolved. The ending of a narrative is called the resolution. In some stories, the narrator or a character leaves readers with a final lesson about life or human experience. More often, however, readers have to figure out the theme on their own by drawing inferences from the end of the story.

IDENTIFICATION AND APPLICATION

- An effective ending brings the story to a satisfying close. It resolves the conflict, ties up loose ends, and may hint at what happens to the characters when the story is over.

  › The way a problem is resolved (the resolution) should be logical and feel like a natural part of the plot, but it can still be a surprise.
  › The resolution should tell clearly how the characters resolved the conflict (or problem)—or how it was resolved for them.
  › At the end of the story, the reader should be able to think about the narrator's role—how his or her point of view affected the way the story was told.
  › The concluding statement may sum up the story and leave readers feeling as if they were thoroughly entertained and thinking "That was a great story!"

- The conclusion might also include a memorable comment from the narrator or a character that helps readers understand the theme—the larger lesson about life or human nature that the story conveyed.

MODEL

In the conclusion to Shirley Jackson's well-known story "The Lottery," readers find out what winning the village lottery entails. Just before the end of the story, the villagers discover that Tessie Hutchinson holds the paper with the black dot. She has "won" the lottery. But winning is losing in this story, and if readers have been paying attention to the events leading up to this point, then they noticed that Tessie doesn't want anyone in her family to be a winner. Something is not quite right here. In the end, the story takes a surprising—even shocking—turn.

"All right, folks," Mr. Summers said. "Let's finish quickly."

Although the villagers had forgotten the ritual and lost the original black box, they still remembered to use stones. The pile of stones the boys had made earlier was ready; there were stones on the ground with the blowing scraps of paper that had come out of the box. Mrs. Delacroix selected a stone so large she had to pick it up with both hands and turned to Mrs. Dunbar. "Come on," she said. "Hurry up."

Mrs. Dunbar had small stones in both hands, and she said, gasping for breath, "I can't run at all. You'll have to go ahead and I'll catch up with you."

The children had stones already, and someone gave little Davy Hutchinson a few pebbles.

Tessie Hutchinson was in the center of a cleared space by now, and she held her hands out desperately as the villagers moved in on her. "It isn't fair," she said. A stone hit her on the side of the head.

Old Man Warner was saying, "Come on, come on, everyone." Steve Adams was in the front of the crowd of villagers, with Mrs. Graves beside him.

"It isn't fair, it isn't right," Mrs. Hutchinson screamed and then they were upon her.

The narrator does not describe exactly what happens to Tessie, but readers can infer that the villagers stone her to death. It's an ugly ending to a story that starts out on a lovely June day. Readers might be horrified to discover what the lottery means. They might also be shocked when they realize that this lottery has taken place every year for generations and is a tradition in the village. The story ends with Tessie crying out, "It isn't fair, it isn't right," a refrain that suggests the danger of blindly following tradition, especially when it leads to unfairness, or injustice. The narrator is completely silent on the matter. Not a character in the text, the narrator is completely detached, just relaying the events without any emotion.

 ## PRACTICE

Write an ending for your story. It should let your readers know how the main character (or characters) resolved the conflict (or problem). Your ending might also hint at what happens to the character after the story is over. In your conclusion (or ending), try to include a thoughtful statement about life or human nature. Your message might be something that the narrator or a character says, or it might be an inference about the theme that the reader can draw from specific evidence in the text.

NOTES

DRAFT

CA-CCSS: CA.RL.7.1, CA.W.7.3a, CA.W.7.3b, CA.W.7.3c, CA.W.7.3d, CA.W.7.3e, CA.W.7.4, CA.W.7.5, CA.W.7.6, CA.W.7.10, CA.SL.7.1a, CA.SL.7.1b, CA.SL.7.1c, CA.SL.7.1d

WRITING PROMPT

Imagine how you would feel if the government banned your favorite TV show. You would probably find it terribly unfair if the authorities took your show off the air. In this unit, you have been reading fiction and nonfiction narratives—imagined and true stories—about characters or real people who do not live in fair, or just, societies. All these selections have something in common: like the gladiators of ancient Rome or the people of North Korea, the characters or people in these texts are the victims of unfair laws and unjust rulers. Think about the principles of an open and just society, and contrast them with the rules of a closed and unjust society. Then write a fictional narrative (or story) about a character who is seeking justice in an unjust society. Model your story on one of the texts you have read in this unit.

Your narrative should include:

- a beginning in which you set the scene
- a clear description of the characters
- a series of clearly described events
- an underlying theme (or message)
- a narrator with a specific point of view

You've already made progress toward writing your own fictional narrative. You've thought about your characters, setting, plot, conflict (or problem), and theme. You've considered your audience and purpose, determined an appropriate text structure to organize your ideas and events, generated plenty of descriptive details, and utilized narrative techniques, such as description, pacing, and dialogue. Now it's time to write a draft of your story.

Use your timeline of events and other graphic organizers to help you as you write. Remember that a fictional narrative has an introduction, a middle, and a conclusion. The introduction (or beginning) gives exposition that establishes the setting, the narrator, the characters, and conflict (or problem) of the story. The middle section, which consists of the rising action, develops the plot by using description, pacing, and dialogue to tell about each event. Transitions connect ideas and events, help the organization (or text structure), and enable readers to follow the flow of events. The conclusion (or ending) tells how the characters resolve their problem, or how it is resolved for them. It ties up loose ends and hints at the theme of the story and its important message. An effective ending can also do more—it can leave a lasting impression on your readers.

When drafting your story, ask yourself these questions:

- How can I improve my introduction to "hook" my readers?
- Who is the narrator of my story? Is it a character from inside or outside the text? How does the narrator's point of view affect the way I tell my story?
- What descriptive details can I add to make my setting, characters, and plot more relevant to my readers?
- Have I ordered the events of the plot so that narrative techniques, such as description, pacing, and dialogue, move the characters and action forward?
- What transition words and phrases can I add to make the order of events clearer?
- Is the end of my story interesting or surprising? Is the resolution of the conflict believable?
- Will my readers understand the theme? What changes can I make to present a clearer theme (or message) to my readers?

Before you submit your draft, read it over carefully. You want to be sure that you have responded to all aspects of the prompt.

NOTES

REVISE

CA-CCSS: CA.RL.7.1, CA.W.7.3a, CA.W.7.3b, CA.W.7.3c, CA.W.7.3d, CA.W.7.3e, CA.W.7.4, CA.W.7.5, CA.W.7.6, CA.SL.7.1a, CA.SL.7.1b, CA.SL.7.1c, CA.SL.7.1d, CA.L.7.3a

WRITING PROMPT

Imagine how you would feel if the government banned your favorite TV show. You would probably find it terribly unfair if the authorities took your show off the air. In this unit, you have been reading fiction and nonfiction narratives—imagined and true stories—about characters or real people who do not live in fair, or just, societies. All these selections have something in common: like the gladiators of ancient Rome or the people of North Korea, the characters or people in these texts are the victims of unfair laws and unjust rulers. Think about the principles of an open and just society, and contrast them with the rules of a closed and unjust society. Then write a fictional narrative (or story) about a character who is seeking justice in an unjust society. Model your story on one of the texts you have read in this unit.

Your narrative should include:

- a beginning in which you set the scene
- a clear description of the characters
- a series of clearly described events
- an underlying theme (or message)
- a narrator with a specific point of view

You have written a draft of your narrative. You have also received input and advice from your peers about how to improve it. Now you are going to revise your draft.

Here are some recommendations to help you revise:

- Review the suggestions made by your peers.

- Focus on your body paragraphs and your use of transitions. Remember: Transitions are words or phrases that help your readers follow the flow of ideas.

  › As you revise, look for places where you can add transition words or phrases to help make the order of events or the relationship between ideas clearer.

  › Test the transitions you have used or want to add. Make sure they reflect the relationship that you want to convey. Review the types of transition words you can use—chronological (sequential or time order), cause-effect, compare-contrast, problem-solution, spatial, order of importance, and so on.

- After you have revised your body paragraphs for transitions, think about whether there is anything else you can do to improve your story's organizational structure.

  › Do you need to reorder any events to make the story clearer or more interesting?

  › Do you need to add an event or provide description so that your readers can better understand the story?

  › Do you need to cut an unnecessary event or description to keep the story from bogging down?

  › Could you change some description to dialogue to pick up the pace of the story?

- As you revise, be aware of how you are using language to express characters' thoughts, words, and actions, along with the events that make up the narrative.

  › Are you varying the types of sentences you're using? Writing becomes boring when it sounds the same. Incorporating a variety of simple, compound, complex, and compound-complex sentences into your writing adds interest.

  › Are you choosing words carefully? Remember that in writing, less is often more. Look for ideas or sentences that you can combine or delete to avoid unnecessary repetition, and make your word choice as precise as it can be.

EDIT, PROOFREAD, AND PUBLISH

CA-CCSS: CA.W.7.3a, CA.W.7.3b, CA.W.7.3c, CA.W.7.3d, CA.W.7.3e, CA.W.7.4, CA.W.7.5, CA.W.7.6, CA.SL.7.1a, CA.SL.7.1b, CA.SL.7.1c, CA.SL.7.1d, CA.SL.7.3, CA.L.7.1a, CA.L.7.1b, CA.L.7.1c, CA.L.7.2a, CA.L.7.2b, CA.L.7.3a, CA.L.7.6

WRITING PROMPT

Imagine how you would feel if the government banned your favorite TV show. You would probably find it terribly unfair if the authorities took your show off the air. In this unit, you have been reading fiction and nonfiction narratives—imagined and true stories—about characters or real people who do not live in fair, or just, societies. All these selections have something in common: like the gladiators of ancient Rome or the people of North Korea, the characters or people in these texts are the victims of unfair laws and unjust rulers. Think about the principles of an open and just society, and contrast them with the rules of a closed and unjust society. Then write a fictional narrative (or story) about a character who is seeking justice in an unjust society. Model your story on one of the texts you have read in this unit.

Your narrative should include:

- a beginning in which you set the scene
- a clear description of the characters
- a series of clearly described events
- an underlying theme (or message)
- a narrator with a specific point of view

You have revised your narrative and received input from your peers on your revised writing. Now it's time to edit and proofread your story to produce a final version. Have you included all the valuable suggestions from your peers? Ask yourself: Have I fully developed my setting, characters, plot, conflict (or problem), and theme? What more can I do to improve my story's descriptive details? Did I do a good job of introducing my story? Did I use transitions well to move from event to event in my body paragraphs? Did I provide an

interesting or surprising ending? Did I use a writing style and tone that matched my story elements of setting, characters, plot, and theme?

When you are satisfied with your work, proofread it for errors. Use this list to check for correct:

- capitalization
- punctuation
- spelling
- grammar
- usage

In addition, check for correct punctuation in the dialogue. Check that you placed a comma correctly after an introductory phrase or clause and that you used a comma to separate a series of coordinate adjectives, such as a *small, pleasant woman.*

Once you have made your corrections to your writing, you are ready to submit and publish your work. You can distribute your story to family and friends, attach it to a bulletin board, or post it to your blog. If you publish online, create links to the stories of injustice that inspired you. That way, readers can read more stories such as the one you wrote.

Text Fulfillment
Through StudySync

If you are interested in specific titles, please fill out the form below and we will check availability through our partners.

ORDER DETAILS

Date:

TITLE	AUTHOR	Paperback/ Hardcover	Specific Edition *If Applicable*	Quantity

SHIPPING INFORMATION

Contact:

Title:

School/District:

Address Line 1:

Address Line 2:

Zip or Postal Code:

Phone:

Mobile:

Email:

BILLING INFORMATION ☐ *SAME AS SHIPPING*

Contact:

Title:

School/District:

Address Line 1:

Address Line 2:

Zip or Postal Code:

Phone:

Mobile:

Email:

PAYMENT INFORMATION

☐ CREDIT CARD

Name on Card:

Card Number:

Expiration Date:

Security Code:

☐ PO

Purchase Order Number:

StudySync Text Fulfillment, BookheadEd Learning, LLC
610 Daniel Young Drive | Sonoma, CA 95476